C-4437 CAREER EXAMINATION SERIES

This is your
PASSBOOK for...

Library Development Assistant

Test Preparation Study Guide
Questions & Answers

NATIONAL LEARNING CORPORATION®

COPYRIGHT NOTICE

This book is SOLELY intended for, is sold ONLY to, and its use is RESTRICTED to individual, bona fide applicants or candidates who qualify by virtue of having seriously filed applications for appropriate license, certificate, professional and/or promotional advancement, higher school matriculation, scholarship, or other legitimate requirements of education and/or governmental authorities.

This book is NOT intended for use, class instruction, tutoring, training, duplication, copying, reprinting, excerption, or adaptation, etc., by:

1) Other publishers
2) Proprietors and/or Instructors of "Coaching" and/or Preparatory Courses
3) Personnel and/or Training Divisions of commercial, industrial, and governmental organizations
4) Schools, colleges, or universities and/or their departments and staffs, including teachers and other personnel
5) Testing Agencies or Bureaus
6) Study groups which seek by the purchase of a single volume to copy and/or duplicate and/or adapt this material for use by the group as a whole without having purchased individual volumes for each of the members of the group
7) Et al.

Such persons would be in violation of appropriate Federal and State statutes.

PROVISION OF LICENSING AGREEMENTS – Recognized educational, commercial, industrial, and governmental institutions and organizations, and others legitimately engaged in educational pursuits, including training, testing, and measurement activities, may address request for a licensing agreement to the copyright owners, who will determine whether, and under what conditions, including fees and charges, the materials in this book may be used them. In other words, a licensing facility exists for the legitimate use of the material in this book on other than an individual basis. However, it is asseverated and affirmed here that the material in this book CANNOT be used without the receipt of the express permission of such a licensing agreement from the Publishers. Inquiries re licensing should be addressed to the company, attention rights and permissions department.

All rights reserved, including the right of reproduction in whole or in part, in any form or by any means, electronic or mechanical, including photocopying, recording, or by any information storage and retrieval system, without permission in writing from the Publisher.

Copyright © 2024 by
National Learning Corporation

212 Michael Drive, Syosset, NY 11791
(516) 921-8888 • www.passbooks.com
E-mail: info@passbooks.com

PASSBOOK® SERIES

THE *PASSBOOK® SERIES* has been created to prepare applicants and candidates for the ultimate academic battlefield – the examination room.

At some time in our lives, each and every one of us may be required to take an examination – for validation, matriculation, admission, qualification, registration, certification, or licensure.

Based on the assumption that every applicant or candidate has met the basic formal educational standards, has taken the required number of courses, and read the necessary texts, the *PASSBOOK® SERIES* furnishes the one special preparation which may assure passing with confidence, instead of failing with insecurity. Examination questions – together with answers – are furnished as the basic vehicle for study so that the mysteries of the examination and its compounding difficulties may be eliminated or diminished by a sure method.

This book is meant to help you pass your examination provided that you qualify and are serious in your objective.

The entire field is reviewed through the huge store of content information which is succinctly presented through a provocative and challenging approach – the question-and-answer method.

A climate of success is established by furnishing the correct answers at the end of each test.

You soon learn to recognize types of questions, forms of questions, and patterns of questioning. You may even begin to anticipate expected outcomes.

You perceive that many questions are repeated or adapted so that you can gain acute insights, which may enable you to score many sure points.

You learn how to confront new questions, or types of questions, and to attack them confidently and work out the correct answers.

You note objectives and emphases, and recognize pitfalls and dangers, so that you may make positive educational adjustments.

Moreover, you are kept fully informed in relation to new concepts, methods, practices, and directions in the field.

You discover that you are actually taking the examination all the time: you are preparing for the examination by "taking" an examination, not by reading extraneous and/or supererogatory textbooks.

In short, this PASSBOOK®, used directedly, should be an important factor in helping you to pass your test.

LIBRARY DEVELOPMENT ASSISTANT

DUTIES
An employee in this class performs fundraising work in a public library. Responsibility is included for researching possible donors and planning fundraising events. The incumbent is expected to use some judgment and initiative in performing duties. The work is performed under the supervision of an administrative superior and is reviewed through conferences and written reports. Performs related work as required.

SCOPE OF THE EXAMINATION
The written test will cover knowledge, skills, and/or abilities in such areas as:
1. Understanding and interpreting written material;
2. Understanding and interpreting tabular material;
3. Preparing written material;
4. Budgeting; and
5. Principles of fundraising and marketing.

HOW TO TAKE A TEST

I. YOU MUST PASS AN EXAMINATION

A. *WHAT EVERY CANDIDATE SHOULD KNOW*

Examination applicants often ask us for help in preparing for the written test. What can I study in advance? What kinds of questions will be asked? How will the test be given? How will the papers be graded?

As an applicant for a civil service examination, you may be wondering about some of these things. Our purpose here is to suggest effective methods of advance study and to describe civil service examinations.

Your chances for success on this examination can be increased if you know how to prepare. Those "pre-examination jitters" can be reduced if you know what to expect. You can even experience an adventure in good citizenship if you know why civil service exams are given.

B. *WHY ARE CIVIL SERVICE EXAMINATIONS GIVEN?*

Civil service examinations are important to you in two ways. As a citizen, you want public jobs filled by employees who know how to do their work. As a job seeker, you want a fair chance to compete for that job on an equal footing with other candidates. The best-known means of accomplishing this two-fold goal is the competitive examination.

Exams are widely publicized throughout the nation. They may be administered for jobs in federal, state, city, municipal, town or village governments or agencies.

Any citizen may apply, with some limitations, such as the age or residence of applicants. Your experience and education may be reviewed to see whether you meet the requirements for the particular examination. When these requirements exist, they are reasonable and applied consistently to all applicants. Thus, a competitive examination may cause you some uneasiness now, but it is your privilege and safeguard.

C. *HOW ARE CIVIL SERVICE EXAMS DEVELOPED?*

Examinations are carefully written by trained technicians who are specialists in the field known as "psychological measurement," in consultation with recognized authorities in the field of work that the test will cover. These experts recommend the subject matter areas or skills to be tested; only those knowledges or skills important to your success on the job are included. The most reliable books and source materials available are used as references. Together, the experts and technicians judge the difficulty level of the questions.

Test technicians know how to phrase questions so that the problem is clearly stated. Their ethics do not permit "trick" or "catch" questions. Questions may have been tried out on sample groups, or subjected to statistical analysis, to determine their usefulness.

Written tests are often used in combination with performance tests, ratings of training and experience, and oral interviews. All of these measures combine to form the best-known means of finding the right person for the right job.

II. HOW TO PASS THE WRITTEN TEST

A. NATURE OF THE EXAMINATION

To prepare intelligently for civil service examinations, you should know how they differ from school examinations you have taken. In school you were assigned certain definite pages to read or subjects to cover. The examination questions were quite detailed and usually emphasized memory. Civil service exams, on the other hand, try to discover your present ability to perform the duties of a position, plus your potentiality to learn these duties. In other words, a civil service exam attempts to predict how successful you will be. Questions cover such a broad area that they cannot be as minute and detailed as school exam questions.

In the public service similar kinds of work, or positions, are grouped together in one "class." This process is known as *position-classification*. All the positions in a class are paid according to the salary range for that class. One class title covers all of these positions, and they are all tested by the same examination.

B. FOUR BASIC STEPS

1) Study the announcement

How, then, can you know what subjects to study? Our best answer is: "Learn as much as possible about the class of positions for which you've applied." The exam will test the knowledge, skills and abilities needed to do the work.

Your most valuable source of information about the position you want is the official exam announcement. This announcement lists the training and experience qualifications. Check these standards and apply only if you come reasonably close to meeting them.

The brief description of the position in the examination announcement offers some clues to the subjects which will be tested. Think about the job itself. Review the duties in your mind. Can you perform them, or are there some in which you are rusty? Fill in the blank spots in your preparation.

Many jurisdictions preview the written test in the exam announcement by including a section called "Knowledge and Abilities Required," "Scope of the Examination," or some similar heading. Here you will find out specifically what fields will be tested.

2) Review your own background

Once you learn in general what the position is all about, and what you need to know to do the work, ask yourself which subjects you already know fairly well and which need improvement. You may wonder whether to concentrate on improving your strong areas or on building some background in your fields of weakness. When the announcement has specified "some knowledge" or "considerable knowledge," or has used adjectives like "beginning principles of..." or "advanced ... methods," you can get a clue as to the number and difficulty of questions to be asked in any given field. More questions, and hence broader coverage, would be included for those subjects which are more important in the work. Now weigh your strengths and weaknesses against the job requirements and prepare accordingly.

3) Determine the level of the position

Another way to tell how intensively you should prepare is to understand the level of the job for which you are applying. Is it the entering level? In other words, is this the position in which beginners in a field of work are hired? Or is it an intermediate or advanced level? Sometimes this is indicated by such words as "Junior" or "Senior" in the class title. Other jurisdictions use Roman numerals to designate the level – Clerk I, Clerk II, for example. The word "Supervisor" sometimes appears in the title. If the level is not indicated by the title, check the description of duties. Will you be working under very close supervision, or will you have responsibility for independent decisions in this work?

4) Choose appropriate study materials

Now that you know the subjects to be examined and the relative amount of each subject to be covered, you can choose suitable study materials. For beginning level jobs, or even advanced ones, if you have a pronounced weakness in some aspect of your training, read a modern, standard textbook in that field. Be sure it is up to date and has general coverage. Such books are normally available at your library, and the librarian will be glad to help you locate one. For entry-level positions, questions of appropriate difficulty are chosen – neither highly advanced questions, nor those too simple. Such questions require careful thought but not advanced training.

If the position for which you are applying is technical or advanced, you will read more advanced, specialized material. If you are already familiar with the basic principles of your field, elementary textbooks would waste your time. Concentrate on advanced textbooks and technical periodicals. Think through the concepts and review difficult problems in your field.

These are all general sources. You can get more ideas on your own initiative, following these leads. For example, training manuals and publications of the government agency which employs workers in your field can be useful, particularly for technical and professional positions. A letter or visit to the government department involved may result in more specific study suggestions, and certainly will provide you with a more definite idea of the exact nature of the position you are seeking.

III. KINDS OF TESTS

Tests are used for purposes other than measuring knowledge and ability to perform specified duties. For some positions, it is equally important to test ability to make adjustments to new situations or to profit from training. In others, basic mental abilities not dependent on information are essential. Questions which test these things may not appear as pertinent to the duties of the position as those which test for knowledge and information. Yet they are often highly important parts of a fair examination. For very general questions, it is almost impossible to help you direct your study efforts. What we can do is to point out some of the more common of these general abilities needed in public service positions and describe some typical questions.

1) General information

Broad, general information has been found useful for predicting job success in some kinds of work. This is tested in a variety of ways, from vocabulary lists to questions about current events. Basic background in some field of work, such as sociology or economics, may be sampled in a group of questions. Often these are principles which have become familiar to most persons through exposure rather than through formal training. It is difficult to advise you how to study for these questions; being alert to the world around you is our best suggestion.

2) Verbal ability

An example of an ability needed in many positions is verbal or language ability. Verbal ability is, in brief, the ability to use and understand words. Vocabulary and grammar tests are typical measures of this ability. Reading comprehension or paragraph interpretation questions are common in many kinds of civil service tests. You are given a paragraph of written material and asked to find its central meaning.

3) Numerical ability

Number skills can be tested by the familiar arithmetic problem, by checking paired lists of numbers to see which are alike and which are different, or by interpreting charts and graphs. In the latter test, a graph may be printed in the test booklet which you are asked to use as the basis for answering questions.

4) Observation

A popular test for law-enforcement positions is the observation test. A picture is shown to you for several minutes, then taken away. Questions about the picture test your ability to observe both details and larger elements.

5) Following directions

In many positions in the public service, the employee must be able to carry out written instructions dependably and accurately. You may be given a chart with several columns, each column listing a variety of information. The questions require you to carry out directions involving the information given in the chart.

6) Skills and aptitudes

Performance tests effectively measure some manual skills and aptitudes. When the skill is one in which you are trained, such as typing or shorthand, you can practice. These tests are often very much like those given in business school or high school courses. For many of the other skills and aptitudes, however, no short-time preparation can be made. Skills and abilities natural to you or that you have developed throughout your lifetime are being tested.

Many of the general questions just described provide all the data needed to answer the questions and ask you to use your reasoning ability to find the answers. Your best preparation for these tests, as well as for tests of facts and ideas, is to be at your physical and mental best. You, no doubt, have your own methods of getting into an exam-taking mood and keeping "in shape." The next section lists some ideas on this subject.

IV. KINDS OF QUESTIONS

Only rarely is the "essay" question, which you answer in narrative form, used in civil service tests. Civil service tests are usually of the short-answer type. Full instructions for answering these questions will be given to you at the examination. But in case this is your first experience with short-answer questions and separate answer sheets, here is what you need to know:

1) Multiple-choice Questions

Most popular of the short-answer questions is the "multiple choice" or "best answer" question. It can be used, for example, to test for factual knowledge, ability to solve problems or judgment in meeting situations found at work.

A multiple-choice question is normally one of three types—
- It can begin with an incomplete statement followed by several possible endings. You are to find the one ending which *best* completes the statement, although some of the others may not be entirely wrong.
- It can also be a complete statement in the form of a question which is answered by choosing one of the statements listed.

- It can be in the form of a problem – again you select the best answer.

Here is an example of a multiple-choice question with a discussion which should give you some clues as to the method for choosing the right answer:

When an employee has a complaint about his assignment, the action which will *best* help him overcome his difficulty is to
   A. discuss his difficulty with his coworkers
   B. take the problem to the head of the organization
   C. take the problem to the person who gave him the assignment
   D. say nothing to anyone about his complaint

In answering this question, you should study each of the choices to find which is best. Consider choice "A" – Certainly an employee may discuss his complaint with fellow employees, but no change or improvement can result, and the complaint remains unresolved. Choice "B" is a poor choice since the head of the organization probably does not know what assignment you have been given, and taking your problem to him is known as "going over the head" of the supervisor. The supervisor, or person who made the assignment, is the person who can clarify it or correct any injustice. Choice "C" is, therefore, correct. To say nothing, as in choice "D," is unwise. Supervisors have and interest in knowing the problems employees are facing, and the employee is seeking a solution to his problem.

2) True/False Questions

The "true/false" or "right/wrong" form of question is sometimes used. Here a complete statement is given. Your job is to decide whether the statement is right or wrong.

SAMPLE: A roaming cell-phone call to a nearby city costs less than a non-roaming call to a distant city.

This statement is wrong, or false, since roaming calls are more expensive.

This is not a complete list of all possible question forms, although most of the others are variations of these common types. You will always get complete directions for answering questions. Be sure you understand *how* to mark your answers – ask questions until you do.

V. RECORDING YOUR ANSWERS

Computer terminals are used more and more today for many different kinds of exams.

For an examination with very few applicants, you may be told to record your answers in the test booklet itself. Separate answer sheets are much more common. If this separate answer sheet is to be scored by machine – and this is often the case – it is highly important that you mark your answers correctly in order to get credit.

An electronic scoring machine is often used in civil service offices because of the speed with which papers can be scored. Machine-scored answer sheets must be marked with a pencil, which will be given to you. This pencil has a high graphite content which responds to the electronic scoring machine. As a matter of fact, stray dots may register as answers, so do not let your pencil rest on the answer sheet while you are pondering the correct answer. Also, if your pencil lead breaks or is otherwise defective, ask for another.

Since the answer sheet will be dropped in a slot in the scoring machine, be careful not to bend the corners or get the paper crumpled.

The answer sheet normally has five vertical columns of numbers, with 30 numbers to a column. These numbers correspond to the question numbers in your test booklet. After each number, going across the page are four or five pairs of dotted lines. These short dotted lines have small letters or numbers above them. The first two pairs may also have a "T" or "F" above the letters. This indicates that the first two pairs only are to be used if the questions are of the true-false type. If the questions are multiple choice, disregard the "T" and "F" and pay attention only to the small letters or numbers.

Answer your questions in the manner of the sample that follows:

32. The largest city in the United States is
    A. Washington, D.C.
    B. New York City
    C. Chicago
    D. Detroit
    E. San Francisco

1) Choose the answer you think is best. (New York City is the largest, so "B" is correct.)
2) Find the row of dotted lines numbered the same as the question you are answering. (Find row number 32)
3) Find the pair of dotted lines corresponding to the answer. (Find the pair of lines under the mark "B.")
4) Make a solid black mark between the dotted lines.

VI. BEFORE THE TEST

Common sense will help you find procedures to follow to get ready for an examination. Too many of us, however, overlook these sensible measures. Indeed, nervousness and fatigue have been found to be the most serious reasons why applicants fail to do their best on civil service tests. Here is a list of reminders:

- Begin your preparation early – Don't wait until the last minute to go scurrying around for books and materials or to find out what the position is all about.
- Prepare continuously – An hour a night for a week is better than an all-night cram session. This has been definitely established. What is more, a night a week for a month will return better dividends than crowding your study into a shorter period of time.
- Locate the place of the exam – You have been sent a notice telling you when and where to report for the examination. If the location is in a different town or otherwise unfamiliar to you, it would be well to inquire the best route and learn something about the building.
- Relax the night before the test – Allow your mind to rest. Do not study at all that night. Plan some mild recreation or diversion; then go to bed early and get a good night's sleep.
- Get up early enough to make a leisurely trip to the place for the test – This way unforeseen events, traffic snarls, unfamiliar buildings, etc. will not upset you.
- Dress comfortably – A written test is not a fashion show. You will be known by number and not by name, so wear something comfortable.

- Leave excess paraphernalia at home – Shopping bags and odd bundles will get in your way. You need bring only the items mentioned in the official notice you received; usually everything you need is provided. Do not bring reference books to the exam. They will only confuse those last minutes and be taken away from you when in the test room.
- Arrive somewhat ahead of time – If because of transportation schedules you must get there very early, bring a newspaper or magazine to take your mind off yourself while waiting.
- Locate the examination room – When you have found the proper room, you will be directed to the seat or part of the room where you will sit. Sometimes you are given a sheet of instructions to read while you are waiting. Do not fill out any forms until you are told to do so; just read them and be prepared.
- Relax and prepare to listen to the instructions
- If you have any physical problem that may keep you from doing your best, be sure to tell the test administrator. If you are sick or in poor health, you really cannot do your best on the exam. You can come back and take the test some other time.

VII. AT THE TEST

The day of the test is here and you have the test booklet in your hand. The temptation to get going is very strong. Caution! There is more to success than knowing the right answers. You must know how to identify your papers and understand variations in the type of short-answer question used in this particular examination. Follow these suggestions for maximum results from your efforts:

1) Cooperate with the monitor

The test administrator has a duty to create a situation in which you can be as much at ease as possible. He will give instructions, tell you when to begin, check to see that you are marking your answer sheet correctly, and so on. He is not there to guard you, although he will see that your competitors do not take unfair advantage. He wants to help you do your best.

2) Listen to all instructions

Don't jump the gun! Wait until you understand all directions. In most civil service tests you get more time than you need to answer the questions. So don't be in a hurry. Read each word of instructions until you clearly understand the meaning. Study the examples, listen to all announcements and follow directions. Ask questions if you do not understand what to do.

3) Identify your papers

Civil service exams are usually identified by number only. You will be assigned a number; you must not put your name on your test papers. Be sure to copy your number correctly. Since more than one exam may be given, copy your exact examination title.

4) Plan your time

Unless you are told that a test is a "speed" or "rate of work" test, speed itself is usually not important. Time enough to answer all the questions will be provided, but this does not mean that you have all day. An overall time limit has been set. Divide the total time (in minutes) by the number of questions to determine the approximate time you have for each question.

5) Do not linger over difficult questions

If you come across a difficult question, mark it with a paper clip (useful to have along) and come back to it when you have been through the booklet. One caution if you do this – be sure to skip a number on your answer sheet as well. Check often to be sure that you have not lost your place and that you are marking in the row numbered the same as the question you are answering.

6) Read the questions

Be sure you know what the question asks! Many capable people are unsuccessful because they failed to *read* the questions correctly.

7) Answer all questions

Unless you have been instructed that a penalty will be deducted for incorrect answers, it is better to guess than to omit a question.

8) Speed tests

It is often better NOT to guess on speed tests. It has been found that on timed tests people are tempted to spend the last few seconds before time is called in marking answers at random – without even reading them – in the hope of picking up a few extra points. To discourage this practice, the instructions may warn you that your score will be "corrected" for guessing. That is, a penalty will be applied. The incorrect answers will be deducted from the correct ones, or some other penalty formula will be used.

9) Review your answers

If you finish before time is called, go back to the questions you guessed or omitted to give them further thought. Review other answers if you have time.

10) Return your test materials

If you are ready to leave before others have finished or time is called, take ALL your materials to the monitor and leave quietly. Never take any test material with you. The monitor can discover whose papers are not complete, and taking a test booklet may be grounds for disqualification.

VIII. EXAMINATION TECHNIQUES

1) Read the general instructions carefully. These are usually printed on the first page of the exam booklet. As a rule, these instructions refer to the timing of the examination; the fact that you should not start work until the signal and must stop work at a signal, etc. If there are any *special* instructions, such as a choice of questions to be answered, make sure that you note this instruction carefully.

2) When you are ready to start work on the examination, that is as soon as the signal has been given, read the instructions to each question booklet, underline any key words or phrases, such as *least, best, outline, describe* and the like. In this way you will tend to answer as requested rather than discover on reviewing your paper that you *listed without describing*, that you selected the *worst* choice rather than the *best* choice, etc.

3) If the examination is of the objective or multiple-choice type – that is, each question will also give a series of possible answers: A, B, C or D, and you are called upon to select the best answer and write the letter next to that answer on your answer paper – it is advisable to start answering each question in turn. There may be anywhere from 50 to 100 such questions in the three or four hours allotted and you can see how much time would be taken if you read through all the questions before beginning to answer any. Furthermore, if you come across a question or group of questions which you know would be difficult to answer, it would undoubtedly affect your handling of all the other questions.

4) If the examination is of the essay type and contains but a few questions, it is a moot point as to whether you should read all the questions before starting to answer any one. Of course, if you are given a choice – say five out of seven and the like – then it is essential to read all the questions so you can eliminate the two that are most difficult. If, however, you are asked to answer all the questions, there may be danger in trying to answer the easiest one first because you may find that you will spend too much time on it. The best technique is to answer the first question, then proceed to the second, etc.

5) Time your answers. Before the exam begins, write down the time it started, then add the time allowed for the examination and write down the time it must be completed, then divide the time available somewhat as follows:
   - If 3-1/2 hours are allowed, that would be 210 minutes. If you have 80 objective-type questions, that would be an average of 2-1/2 minutes per question. Allow yourself no more than 2 minutes per question, or a total of 160 minutes, which will permit about 50 minutes to review.
   - If for the time allotment of 210 minutes there are 7 essay questions to answer, that would average about 30 minutes a question. Give yourself only 25 minutes per question so that you have about 35 minutes to review.

6) The most important instruction is to *read each question* and make sure you know what is wanted. The second most important instruction is to *time yourself properly* so that you answer every question. The third most important instruction is to *answer every question*. Guess if you have to but include something for each question. Remember that you will receive no credit for a blank and will probably receive some credit if you write something in answer to an essay question. If you guess a letter – say "B" for a multiple-choice question – you may have guessed right. If you leave a blank as an answer to a multiple-choice question, the examiners may respect your feelings but it will not add a point to your score. Some exams may penalize you for wrong answers, so in such cases *only*, you may not want to guess unless you have some basis for your answer.

7) Suggestions
   a. Objective-type questions
      1. Examine the question booklet for proper sequence of pages and questions
      2. Read all instructions carefully
      3. Skip any question which seems too difficult; return to it after all other questions have been answered
      4. Apportion your time properly; do not spend too much time on any single question or group of questions

5. Note and underline key words – *all, most, fewest, least, best, worst, same, opposite,* etc.
6. Pay particular attention to negatives
7. Note unusual option, e.g., unduly long, short, complex, different or similar in content to the body of the question
8. Observe the use of "hedging" words – *probably, may, most likely,* etc.
9. Make sure that your answer is put next to the same number as the question
10. Do not second-guess unless you have good reason to believe the second answer is definitely more correct
11. Cross out original answer if you decide another answer is more accurate; do not erase until you are ready to hand your paper in
12. Answer all questions; guess unless instructed otherwise
13. Leave time for review

   b. Essay questions
      1. Read each question carefully
      2. Determine exactly what is wanted. Underline key words or phrases.
      3. Decide on outline or paragraph answer
      4. Include many different points and elements unless asked to develop any one or two points or elements
      5. Show impartiality by giving pros and cons unless directed to select one side only
      6. Make and write down any assumptions you find necessary to answer the questions
      7. Watch your English, grammar, punctuation and choice of words
      8. Time your answers; don't crowd material

8) Answering the essay question

Most essay questions can be answered by framing the specific response around several key words or ideas. Here are a few such key words or ideas:

M's: manpower, materials, methods, money, management
P's: purpose, program, policy, plan, procedure, practice, problems, pitfalls, personnel, public relations

   a. Six basic steps in handling problems:
      1. Preliminary plan and background development
      2. Collect information, data and facts
      3. Analyze and interpret information, data and facts
      4. Analyze and develop solutions as well as make recommendations
      5. Prepare report and sell recommendations
      6. Install recommendations and follow up effectiveness

   b. Pitfalls to avoid
      1. *Taking things for granted* – A statement of the situation does not necessarily imply that each of the elements is necessarily true; for example, a complaint may be invalid and biased so that all that can be taken for granted is that a complaint has been registered

2. *Considering only one side of a situation* – Wherever possible, indicate several alternatives and then point out the reasons you selected the best one
3. *Failing to indicate follow up* – Whenever your answer indicates action on your part, make certain that you will take proper follow-up action to see how successful your recommendations, procedures or actions turn out to be
4. *Taking too long in answering any single question* – Remember to time your answers properly

IX. AFTER THE TEST

Scoring procedures differ in detail among civil service jurisdictions although the general principles are the same. Whether the papers are hand-scored or graded by machine we have described, they are nearly always graded by number. That is, the person who marks the paper knows only the number – never the name – of the applicant. Not until all the papers have been graded will they be matched with names. If other tests, such as training and experience or oral interview ratings have been given, scores will be combined. Different parts of the examination usually have different weights. For example, the written test might count 60 percent of the final grade, and a rating of training and experience 40 percent. In many jurisdictions, veterans will have a certain number of points added to their grades.

After the final grade has been determined, the names are placed in grade order and an eligible list is established. There are various methods for resolving ties between those who get the same final grade – probably the most common is to place first the name of the person whose application was received first. Job offers are made from the eligible list in the order the names appear on it. You will be notified of your grade and your rank as soon as all these computations have been made. This will be done as rapidly as possible.

People who are found to meet the requirements in the announcement are called "eligibles." Their names are put on a list of eligible candidates. An eligible's chances of getting a job depend on how high he stands on this list and how fast agencies are filling jobs from the list.

When a job is to be filled from a list of eligibles, the agency asks for the names of people on the list of eligibles for that job. When the civil service commission receives this request, it sends to the agency the names of the three people highest on this list. Or, if the job to be filled has specialized requirements, the office sends the agency the names of the top three persons who meet these requirements from the general list.

The appointing officer makes a choice from among the three people whose names were sent to him. If the selected person accepts the appointment, the names of the others are put back on the list to be considered for future openings.

That is the rule in hiring from all kinds of eligible lists, whether they are for typist, carpenter, chemist, or something else. For every vacancy, the appointing officer has his choice of any one of the top three eligibles on the list. This explains why the person whose name is on top of the list sometimes does not get an appointment when some of the persons lower on the list do. If the appointing officer chooses the second or third eligible, the No. 1 eligible does not get a job at once, but stays on the list until he is appointed or the list is terminated.

X. HOW TO PASS THE INTERVIEW TEST

The examination for which you applied requires an oral interview test. You have already taken the written test and you are now being called for the interview test – the final part of the formal examination.

You may think that it is not possible to prepare for an interview test and that there are no procedures to follow during an interview. Our purpose is to point out some things you can do in advance that will help you and some good rules to follow and pitfalls to avoid while you are being interviewed.

What is an interview supposed to test?

The written examination is designed to test the technical knowledge and competence of the candidate; the oral is designed to evaluate intangible qualities, not readily measured otherwise, and to establish a list showing the relative fitness of each candidate – as measured against his competitors – for the position sought. Scoring is not on the basis of "right" and "wrong," but on a sliding scale of values ranging from "not passable" to "outstanding." As a matter of fact, it is possible to achieve a relatively low score without a single "incorrect" answer because of evident weakness in the qualities being measured.

Occasionally, an examination may consist entirely of an oral test – either an individual or a group oral. In such cases, information is sought concerning the technical knowledges and abilities of the candidate, since there has been no written examination for this purpose. More commonly, however, an oral test is used to supplement a written examination.

Who conducts interviews?

The composition of oral boards varies among different jurisdictions. In nearly all, a representative of the personnel department serves as chairman. One of the members of the board may be a representative of the department in which the candidate would work. In some cases, "outside experts" are used, and, frequently, a businessman or some other representative of the general public is asked to serve. Labor and management or other special groups may be represented. The aim is to secure the services of experts in the appropriate field.

However the board is composed, it is a good idea (and not at all improper or unethical) to ascertain in advance of the interview who the members are and what groups they represent. When you are introduced to them, you will have some idea of their backgrounds and interests, and at least you will not stutter and stammer over their names.

What should be done before the interview?

While knowledge about the board members is useful and takes some of the surprise element out of the interview, there is other preparation which is more substantive. It *is* possible to prepare for an oral interview – in several ways:

1) Keep a copy of your application and review it carefully before the interview

This may be the only document before the oral board, and the starting point of the interview. Know what education and experience you have listed there, and the sequence and dates of all of it. Sometimes the board will ask you to review the highlights of your experience for them; you should not have to hem and haw doing it.

2) Study the class specification and the examination announcement

Usually, the oral board has one or both of these to guide them. The qualities, characteristics or knowledges required by the position sought are stated in these documents. They offer valuable clues as to the nature of the oral interview. For example, if the job involves supervisory responsibilities, the announcement will usually indicate that knowledge of modern supervisory methods and the qualifications of the candidate as a supervisor will be tested. If so, you can expect such questions, frequently in the form of a hypothetical situation which you are expected to solve. NEVER go into an oral without knowledge of the duties and responsibilities of the job you seek.

3) Think through each qualification required

Try to visualize the kind of questions you would ask if you were a board member. How well could you answer them? Try especially to appraise your own knowledge and background in each area, *measured against the job sought*, and identify any areas in which you are weak. Be critical and realistic – do not flatter yourself.

4) Do some general reading in areas in which you feel you may be weak

For example, if the job involves supervision and your past experience has NOT, some general reading in supervisory methods and practices, particularly in the field of human relations, might be useful. Do NOT study agency procedures or detailed manuals. The oral board will be testing your understanding and capacity, not your memory.

5) Get a good night's sleep and watch your general health and mental attitude

You will want a clear head at the interview. Take care of a cold or any other minor ailment, and of course, no hangovers.

What should be done on the day of the interview?

Now comes the day of the interview itself. Give yourself plenty of time to get there. Plan to arrive somewhat ahead of the scheduled time, particularly if your appointment is in the fore part of the day. If a previous candidate fails to appear, the board might be ready for you a bit early. By early afternoon an oral board is almost invariably behind schedule if there are many candidates, and you may have to wait. Take along a book or magazine to read, or your application to review, but leave any extraneous material in the waiting room when you go in for your interview. In any event, relax and compose yourself.

The matter of dress is important. The board is forming impressions about you – from your experience, your manners, your attitude, and your appearance. Give your personal appearance careful attention. Dress your best, but not your flashiest. Choose conservative, appropriate clothing, and be sure it is immaculate. This is a business interview, and your appearance should indicate that you regard it as such. Besides, being well groomed and properly dressed will help boost your confidence.

Sooner or later, someone will call your name and escort you into the interview room. *This is it.* From here on you are on your own. It is too late for any more preparation. But remember, you asked for this opportunity to prove your fitness, and you are here because your request was granted.

What happens when you go in?

The usual sequence of events will be as follows: The clerk (who is often the board stenographer) will introduce you to the chairman of the oral board, who will introduce you to the other members of the board. Acknowledge the introductions before you sit down. Do not be surprised if you find a microphone facing you or a stenotypist sitting by. Oral interviews are usually recorded in the event of an appeal or other review.

Usually the chairman of the board will open the interview by reviewing the highlights of your education and work experience from your application – primarily for the benefit of the other members of the board, as well as to get the material into the record. Do not interrupt or comment unless there is an error or significant misinterpretation; if that is the case, do not hesitate. But do not quibble about insignificant matters. Also, he will usually ask you some question about your education, experience or your present job – partly to get you to start talking and to establish the interviewing "rapport." He may start the actual questioning, or turn it over to one of the other members. Frequently, each member undertakes the questioning on a particular area, one in which he is perhaps most competent, so you can expect each member to participate in the examination. Because time is limited, you may also expect some rather abrupt switches in the direction the questioning takes, so do not be upset by it. Normally, a board member will not pursue a single line of questioning unless he discovers a particular strength or weakness.

After each member has participated, the chairman will usually ask whether any member has any further questions, then will ask you if you have anything you wish to add. Unless you are expecting this question, it may floor you. Worse, it may start you off on an extended, extemporaneous speech. The board is not usually seeking more information. The question is principally to offer you a last opportunity to present further qualifications or to indicate that you have nothing to add. So, if you feel that a significant qualification or characteristic has been overlooked, it is proper to point it out in a sentence or so. Do not compliment the board on the thoroughness of their examination – they have been sketchy, and you know it. If you wish, merely say, "No thank you, I have nothing further to add." This is a point where you can "talk yourself out" of a good impression or fail to present an important bit of information. Remember, *you close the interview yourself.*

The chairman will then say, "That is all, Mr. _____, thank you." Do not be startled; the interview is over, and quicker than you think. Thank him, gather your belongings and take your leave. Save your sigh of relief for the other side of the door.

How to put your best foot forward

Throughout this entire process, you may feel that the board individually and collectively is trying to pierce your defenses, seek out your hidden weaknesses and embarrass and confuse you. Actually, this is not true. They are obliged to make an appraisal of your qualifications for the job you are seeking, and they want to see you in your best light. Remember, they must interview all candidates and a non-cooperative candidate may become a failure in spite of their best efforts to bring out his qualifications. Here are 15 suggestions that will help you:

1) Be natural – Keep your attitude confident, not cocky

If you are not confident that you can do the job, do not expect the board to be. Do not apologize for your weaknesses, try to bring out your strong points. The board is interested in a positive, not negative, presentation. Cockiness will antagonize any board member and make him wonder if you are covering up a weakness by a false show of strength.

2) Get comfortable, but don't lounge or sprawl

Sit erectly but not stiffly. A careless posture may lead the board to conclude that you are careless in other things, or at least that you are not impressed by the importance of the occasion. Either conclusion is natural, even if incorrect. Do not fuss with your clothing, a pencil or an ashtray. Your hands may occasionally be useful to emphasize a point; do not let them become a point of distraction.

3) Do not wisecrack or make small talk

This is a serious situation, and your attitude should show that you consider it as such. Further, the time of the board is limited – they do not want to waste it, and neither should you.

4) Do not exaggerate your experience or abilities

In the first place, from information in the application or other interviews and sources, the board may know more about you than you think. Secondly, you probably will not get away with it. An experienced board is rather adept at spotting such a situation, so do not take the chance.

5) If you know a board member, do not make a point of it, yet do not hide it

Certainly you are not fooling him, and probably not the other members of the board. Do not try to take advantage of your acquaintanceship – it will probably do you little good.

6) Do not dominate the interview

Let the board do that. They will give you the clues – do not assume that you have to do all the talking. Realize that the board has a number of questions to ask you, and do not try to take up all the interview time by showing off your extensive knowledge of the answer to the first one.

7) Be attentive

You only have 20 minutes or so, and you should keep your attention at its sharpest throughout. When a member is addressing a problem or question to you, give him your undivided attention. Address your reply principally to him, but do not exclude the other board members.

8) Do not interrupt

A board member may be stating a problem for you to analyze. He will ask you a question when the time comes. Let him state the problem, and wait for the question.

9) Make sure you understand the question

Do not try to answer until you are sure what the question is. If it is not clear, restate it in your own words or ask the board member to clarify it for you. However, do not haggle about minor elements.

10) Reply promptly but not hastily

A common entry on oral board rating sheets is "candidate responded readily," or "candidate hesitated in replies." Respond as promptly and quickly as you can, but do not jump to a hasty, ill-considered answer.

11) Do not be peremptory in your answers

A brief answer is proper – but do not fire your answer back. That is a losing game from your point of view. The board member can probably ask questions much faster than you can answer them.

12) Do not try to create the answer you think the board member wants

He is interested in what kind of mind you have and how it works – not in playing games. Furthermore, he can usually spot this practice and will actually grade you down on it.

13) Do not switch sides in your reply merely to agree with a board member

Frequently, a member will take a contrary position merely to draw you out and to see if you are willing and able to defend your point of view. Do not start a debate, yet do not surrender a good position. If a position is worth taking, it is worth defending.

14) Do not be afraid to admit an error in judgment if you are shown to be wrong
The board knows that you are forced to reply without any opportunity for careful consideration. Your answer may be demonstrably wrong. If so, admit it and get on with the interview.

15) Do not dwell at length on your present job
The opening question may relate to your present assignment. Answer the question but do not go into an extended discussion. You are being examined for a *new* job, not your present one. As a matter of fact, try to phrase ALL your answers in terms of the job for which you are being examined.

Basis of Rating
Probably you will forget most of these "do's" and "don'ts" when you walk into the oral interview room. Even remembering them all will not ensure you a passing grade. Perhaps you did not have the qualifications in the first place. But remembering them will help you to put your best foot forward, without treading on the toes of the board members.

Rumor and popular opinion to the contrary notwithstanding, an oral board wants you to make the best appearance possible. They know you are under pressure – but they also want to see how you respond to it as a guide to what your reaction would be under the pressures of the job you seek. They will be influenced by the degree of poise you display, the personal traits you show and the manner in which you respond.

ABOUT THIS BOOK

This book contains tests divided into Examination Sections. Go through each test, answering every question in the margin. We have also attached a sample answer sheet at the back of the book that can be removed and used. At the end of each test look at the answer key and check your answers. On the ones you got wrong, look at the right answer choice and learn. Do not fill in the answers first. Do not memorize the questions and answers, but understand the answer and principles involved. On your test, the questions will likely be different from the samples. Questions are changed and new ones added. If you understand these past questions you should have success with any changes that arise. Tests may consist of several types of questions. We have additional books on each subject should more study be advisable or necessary for you. Finally, the more you study, the better prepared you will be. This book is intended to be the last thing you study before you walk into the examination room. Prior study of relevant texts is also recommended. NLC publishes some of these in our Fundamental Series. Knowledge and good sense are important factors in passing your exam. Good luck also helps. So now study this Passbook, absorb the material contained within and take that knowledge into the examination. Then do your best to pass that exam.

EXAMINATION SECTION

EXAMINATION SECTION
TEST 1

DIRECTIONS: Each question or incomplete statement is followed by several suggested answers or completions. Select the one that BEST answers the question or completes the statement. *PRINT THE LETTER OF THE CORRECT ANSWER IN THE SPACE AT THE RIGHT.*

1. The budget which shows the money to be spent to build and equip a new hospital is known as the _____ budget.   1._____

    A. capital   B. expense   C. planned   D. program

2. A significant characteristic of the program budget is that it lends itself to review and analysis.   2._____
   Why?

    A. The budget has a built-in accounting system that makes close control possible.
    B. The budget includes measurable objectives.
    C. It is possible to review performance based on units of service.
    D. All of the above

3. The advantages of program budgeting over line item and performance budgeting is: 3._____
    I. Tight, administrative control
    II. Forces the administrator to think through his total operation
    III. Measurable objectives
    IV. Simplicity of development
    V. Closer estimates of future costs
   The CORRECT answer is:

    A. I, II   B. II, III, IV
    C. II, III, V   D. III, IV, V

4. Of the following considerations, the one which is LEAST important in preparing a department budget request is the   4._____

    A. amounts in previous budget requests
    B. cost of material
    C. cost of personnel
    D. goals of the agency

5. The type of budget which provides the MOST flexibility in the use of appropriate funds is the _____ budget.   5._____

    A. accrual   B. item   C. line   D. program

6. A WEAKNESS of many budgetary systems today is that they   6._____

    A. are subjectively determined by those most directly involved
    B. focus on management weakness rather than management strength
    C. only show variable costs
    D. show in detail why losses are occurring

7. Standards on which budgets are developed should be based PRIMARILY on

   A. a general consensus
   B. agency wishes
   C. analytical studies
   D. historical performance

8. The income, cost, and expense goals making up a budget are aimed at achieving a pre-determined objective but do not necessarily measure the lowest possible costs.
   This is PRIMARILY so because

   A. budget committees are accounting-oriented and are not sympathetic with the supervisor's personnel problems
   B. budget committees fail to recognize the difference between direct and indirect costs
   C. the level of expenditures provided for in a budget by budget committees is frequently an arbitrary rather than a scientifically determined amount
   D. budget committees spend considerable time evaluating data to the point that the material gathered is not representative or current

9. You, as a unit head, have been asked to submit budget estimates of staff, equipment, and supplies in terms of programs for your unit for the coming fiscal year.
   In addition to their use in planning, such unit budget estimates can be BEST used to

   A. reveal excessive costs in operations
   B. justify increases in the debt limit
   C. analyze employee salary adjustments
   D. predict the success of future programs

10. Which of the following is the BEST reason for budgeting a new calculating machine for an office?

    A. The clerks in the office often make mistakes in adding.
    B. The machine would save time and money.
    C. It was budgeted last year but never received.
    D. All the other offices have calculating machines.

11. As an aspect of the managerial function, a budget is described BEST as a

    A. set of qualitative management controls over productivity
    B. tool based on historical accounting reports
    C. type of management plan expressed in quantitative terms
    D. precise estimate of future quantitative and qualitative contingencies

12. Which one of the following is *generally* accepted as the MAJOR immediate advantage of installing a system of program budgeting? It

    A. encourages managers to relate their decisions to the agency's long-range goals
    B. is a replacement for the financial or fiscal budget
    C. decreases the need for managers to make trade-offs in the decision-making process
    D. helps to adjust budget figures to provide for unexpected developments

13. Of the following, the BEST means for assuring necessary responsiveness of a budgetary program to changing conditions is by

    A. overestimating budgetary expenditures by 15% and assigning the excess to unforeseen problem areas
    B. underestimating budgetary expenditures by at least 20% and setting aside a reserve account in the same amount
    C. reviewing and revising the budget at regular intervals so that it retains its character as a current document
    D. establishing *budget by exception* policies for each division in the agency

14. According to expert thought in the area of budgeting, participation in the preparation of a government agency's budget should GENERALLY involve

    A. only top management
    B. only lower levels of management
    C. all levels of the organization
    D. only a central budget office or bureau

15. Of the following, the MOST useful guide to analysis of budget estimates for the coming fiscal year is a comparison with

    A. appropriations as amended for the current fiscal year
    B. manpower requirements for the previous two years
    C. initial appropriations for the current fiscal year
    D. budget estimates for the preceding five years,

16. Line managers often request more funds for their units than are actually required to attain their current objectives.
    Which one of the following is the MOST important reason for such inflated budget requests? The

    A. expectation that budget examiners will exercise their prerogative of budget cutting
    B. line manager's interest in improving the performance of his unit is thereby indicated to top management
    C. expectation that such requests will make it easier to obtain additional funds in future years
    D. opinion that it makes sense to obtain additional funds and decide later how to use them

17. Integrating budgeting with program planning and evaluation in a city agency is GENERALLY considered to be

    A. *undesirable*; budgeting must focus on the fiscal year at hand, whereas planning must concern itself with developments over a period of years
    B. *desirable*; budgeting facilitates the choice-making process by evaluating the financial implications of agency programs and forcing cost comparisons among them
    C. *undesirable*; accountants and statisticians with the required budgetary skills have little familiarity with the substantive programs that the agency is conducting
    D. *desirable*; such a partnership increases the budgetary skills of planners, thus promoting more effective use of public resources

18. In government budgeting, the problem of relating financial transactions to the fiscal year in which they are budgeted is BEST met by

    A. determining the cash balance by comparing how much money has been received and how much has been paid out
    B. applying net revenue to the fiscal year in which they are collected as offset by relevant expenses
    C. adopting a system whereby appropriations are entered when they are received and expenditures are entered when they are paid out
    D. entering expenditures on the books when the obligation to make the expenditure is made

19. If the agency's bookkeeping system records income when it is received and expenditures when the money is paid out, this system is USUALLY known as a _____ system.

    A. cash
    B. flow-payment
    C. deferred
    D. fiscal year income

20. An audit, as the term applies to budget execution, is MOST NEARLY a

    A. procedure based on the budget estimates
    B. control exercised by the executive on the legislature in the establishment of program priorities
    C. check on the legality of expenditures and is based on the appropriations act
    D. requirement which must be met before funds can be spent

21. In government budgeting, there is a procedure known as *allotment.*
    Of the following statements which relate to allotment, select the one that is MOST generally considered to be correct. Allotment

    A. increases the practice of budget units coming back to the legislative branch for supplemental appropriations
    B. is simply an example of red tape
    C. eliminates the requirement of timing of expenditures
    D. is designed to prevent waste

22. In government budgeting, the establishment of the schedules of allotments is MOST generally the responsibility of the

    A. budget unit and the legislature
    B. budget unit and the executive
    C. budget unit only
    D. executive and the legislature

23. Of the following statements relating to preparation of an organization's budget request, which is the MOST generally valid precaution?

    A. Give specific instructions on the format of budget requests and required supporting data.
    B. Because of the complexity of preparing a budget request, avoid argumentation to support the requests
    C. Put requests in whatever format is desirable.
    D. Consider that final approval will be given to initial estimates.

Question 24.

DIRECTIONS: Answer Question 24 on the basis of the following information.

Sample Budget

Environmental Safety
   Air Pollution Protection
      Personal Services $20,000,000
      Contractual Services   4,000,000
      Supplies and Materials   4,000,000
      Capital Outlay   2,000,000
        Total Air Pollution Protection $30,000,000

   Water Pollution Protection
      Personal Services $23,000,000
      Supplies and Materials   4,500,000
      Capital Outlay   20,500,000
        Total Water Pollution Protection $48,000,000
Total Environmental Safety $78,000,000

24. Based on the above budget, which is the MOST valid statement? 24.____

   A. Environmental Safety, Air Pollution Protection, and Water Pollution Protection could all be considered program elements.
   B. The object listings included water pollution protection and capital outlay.
   C. Examples of the program element listings in the above are personal services and supplies and materials.
   D. Contractual Services and Environmental Safety were the program element listings.

25. Which of the following is NOT an advantage of a program budget over a line-item budget? 25.____
A program budget

   A. allows us to set up priority lists in deciding what activities we will spend our money on
   B. gives us more control over expenditures than a line-item budget
   C. is more informative in that we know the broad purposes of spending money
   D. enables us to see if one program is getting much less money than the others

26. Of the following statements which relate to the budget process in a well-organized government, select the one that is MOST NEARLY correct. 26.____

   A. The budget cycle is the step-by-step process which is repeated each and every fiscal year.
   B. Securing approval of the budget does not take place within the budget cycle.
   C. The development of a new budget and putting it into effect is a two-step process known as the budget cycle.
   D. The fiscal period, usually a fiscal year, has no relation to the budget cycle.

27. If a manager were asked what PPBS stands for, he would be right if he said

   A. public planning budgeting system
   B. planning programming budgeting system
   C. planning projections budgeting system
   D. programming procedures budgeting system

Questions 28-29

DIRECTIONS: Answer Questions 28 and 29 on the basis of the following information.

Sample Budget

	Amount
Refuse Collection	
Personal Services	$ 30,000
Contractual Services	5,000
Supplies and Materials	5,000
Capital Outlay	10,000
	$ 50,000
Residential Collections	
Dwellings – 1 pickup per week	1,000
Tons of refuse collected per year	375
Cost of collections per ton	$ 8
Cost per dwelling pickup per year	$ 3
Total annual cost	$ 3,000

28. The sample budget shown is a simplified example of a _____ budget.

   A. factorial   B. performance
   C. qualitative   D. rational

29. The budget shown in the sample differs CHIEFLY from line-item and program budgets in that it includes

   A. objects of expenditure but not activities or functions
   B. only activities, functions, and controls
   C. activities and functions, but not objects of expenditure
   D. levels of service

30. Performance budgeting focuses PRIMARY attention upon which one of the following? The

   A. things to be acquired, such as supplies and equipment
   B. general character and relative importance of the work to be done or the service to be rendered
   C. list of personnel to be employed, by specific title
   D. separation of employee performance evaluations from employee compensation

KEY (CORRECT ANSWERS)

1.	A	16.	A
2.	B	17.	B
3.	C	18.	D
4.	A	19.	A
5.	D	20.	C
6.	A	21.	D
7.	C	22.	C
8.	C	23.	A
9.	A	24.	A
10.	B	25.	B
11.	C	26.	A
12.	A	27.	B
13.	C	28.	B
14.	C	29.	D
15.	A	30.	B

TEST 2

DIRECTIONS: Each question or incomplete statement is followed by several suggested answers or completions. Select the one that BEST answers the question or completes the statement. *PRINT THE LETTER OF THE CORRECT ANSWER IN THE SPACE AT THE RIGHT.*

1. Of the following, the FIRST step in the installation and operation of a performance budgeting system generally should be the

   A. identification of program costs in relationship to the accounting system and operating structure
   B. identification of the specific end results of past programs in other jurisdictions
   C. identification of work programs that are meaningful for management purposes
   D. establishment of organizational structures each containing only one work program

2. Of the following, the MOST important purpose of a system of quarterly allotments of appropriated funds generally is to enable the

   A. head of the judicial branch to determine the legality of agency requests for budget increases
   B. operating agencies of government to upgrade the quality of their services without increasing costs
   C. head of the executive branch to control the rate at which the operating agencies obligate and expend funds
   D. operating agencies of government to avoid payment for services which have not been properly rendered by employees

3. In the preparation of the agency's budget, the agency's central budget office has two responsibilities: program review and management improvement.
   Which one of the following questions concerning an operating agency's program is MOST closely related to the agency budget officer's program review responsibility?

   A. Can expenditures for supplies, materials, or equipment be reduced?
   B. Will improved work methods contribute to a more effective program?
   C. What is the relative importance of this program as compared with other programs?
   D. Will a realignment of responsibilities contribute to a higher level of program performance?

Questions 4-9.

DIRECTIONS: Questions 4 through 9 are to be answered only on the basis of the information contained in the charts below which relate to the budget allocations of City X, a small suburban community. The charts depict the annual budget allocations by Department and by Expenditures over a five-year period.

CITY X BUDGET IN MILLIONS OF DOLLARS

TABLE I. Budget Allocations by Department

Department	2017	2018	2019	2020	2021
Public Safety	30	45	50	40	50
Health and Welfare	50	75	90	60	70
Engineering	5	8	10	5	8
Human Resources	10	12	20	10	22
Conservation and Environment	10	15	20	20	15
Education and Development	15	25	35	15	15
TOTAL BUDGET	120	180	225	150	180

TABLE II. Budget Allocations by Expenditures

Category	2017	2018	2019	2020	2021
Raw Materials and Machinery	36	63	68	30	98
Capital Outlay	12	27	56	15	18
Personal Services	72	90	101	105	64
TOTAL BUDGET	120	180	225	150	160

4. The year in which the SMALLEST percentage of the total annual budget was allocated to the Department of Education and Development is

   A. 2017   B. 2018   C. 2020   D. 2021

5. Assume that in 2020 the Department of Conservation and Environment divided its annual budget into the three categories of expenditures and in exactly the same proportion as the budget shown in Table II for the year 2020. The amount allocated for capital outlay in the Department of Conservation and Environment's 2020 budget was MOST NEARLY _____ million.

   A. $2   B. $4   C. $6   D. $10

6. From the year 2018 to the year 2020, the sum of the annual budgets for the Departments of Public Safety and Engineering showed an overall _____ million.

   A. decline of $8   B. increase of $7
   C. decline of $15   D. increase of $22

7. The LARGEST dollar increase in departmental budget allocations from one year to the next was in

   A. Public Safety from 2017 to 2018
   B. Health and Welfare from 2017 to 2018
   C. Education and Development from 2019 to 2020
   D. Human Resources from 2019 to 2020

8. During the five-year period, the annual budget of the Department of Human Resources was greater than the annual budget for the Department of Conservation and Environment in _____ of the years.

   A. none   B. one   C. two   D. three

9. If the total City X budget increases at the same rate from 2021 to 2022 as it did from 2020 to 2021, the total City X budget for 2022 will be MOST NEARLY _____ million.

   A. $180 B. $200 C. $210 D. $215

10. The one of the following which is LEAST important in developing a budget for the next fiscal year for project maintenance is the

   A. adequacy of the current year's budget
   B. changes in workload that can be anticipated
   C. budget restrictions indicated in a memorandum covering budget preparations
   D. staff reassignments which are expected during the next fiscal year

11. The performance budget used by the department places MOST emphasis on

   A. building facilities
   B. equipment costs
   C. personnel costs
   D. services rendered

12. The LARGEST part of the expenditures of the department is for

   A. equipment
   B. maintenance
   C. operating materials
   D. personnel services

13. The department function which requires the GREATEST expenditure of funds is

   A. refuse collection
   B. refuse disposal
   C. snow removal
   D. street cleaning

14. A FIRST step in budget preparation is *usually*

   A. a realistic attempt to satisfy all unit requests
   B. forecasting the amount of various kinds of work to be done during the coming budget year
   C. an effort to increase work output
   D. appraising the quality of work done in the previous year

15. There are various types of budgets which are used to measure different government activities.
    The type of budget which *particularly* measures input of resource as compared with output of service is the _____ budget.

   A. capital B. traditional C. performance D. program

16. The budget for a given cost during a given period was $100,000. The actual cost for the period was $90,000. Based upon these facts, one should say that the responsible manager has done a better than expected job in controlling the cost if the cost is

   A. variable and actual production equaled budgeted production
   B. a discretionary fixed cost and actual production equaled budgeted production
   C. variable and actual production was 90% of budgeted production
   D. variable and actual production was 80% of budgeted production

17. In most municipal budgeting systems involving capital and operating budgets, the leasing or renting of facilities is usually shown in

    A. the operating budget
    B. the capital budget
    C. a separate schedule
    D. either budget

18. New York City's budgeting procedure is unusual in that budget appropriations are considered in two parts, as follows: _____ budget and _____ budget.

    A. capital; income
    B. expense; income
    C. revenue; expense
    D. expense; capital

19. Budget planning is MOST useful when it achieves

    A. cost control
    B. forecast of receipts
    C. performance review
    D. personnel reduction

20. After a budget has been developed, it serves to

    A. assist the accounting department in posting expenditures
    B. measure the effectiveness of department managers
    C. provide a yardstick against which actual costs are measured
    D. provide the operating department with total expenditures to date

21. A budget is a plan whereby a goal is set for future operations. It affords a medium for comparing actual expenditures with planned expenditures.
    The one of the following which is the MOST accurate statement on the basis of this statement is that

    A. the budget serves as an accurate measure of past as well as future expenditures
    B. the budget presents an estimate of expenditures to be made in the future
    C. budget estimates should be based upon past budget requirements
    D. planned expenditures usually fall short of actual expenditures

22. If one attempts to list the advantages of the management-by-exception principle as it is used in connection with the budgeting process, several distinct advantages could be cited.
    Which of the following is NOT an advantage of this principle as it applies to the budgeting process? Management-by-exception

    A. saves time
    B. identifies critical problem areas
    C. focuses attention and concentrates effort
    D. escalates the frequency and importance of budget-related decisions

23. Of the following statements that relate to a budget, select the one that is MOST accurate.

    A. A budget is made up by an organization to plan its future activities.
    B. A budget specifies how much the organization to which it relates estimates it will spend over a certain period of time.
    C. A budget specifies in dollars and cents how much is spent in a particular time period.
    D. All plans dealing with money are budgets.

24. Of the following, the one which is NOT a contribution that a budget makes to organizational programming is that a budget

    A. enables a comparison of what actually happened with what was expected
    B. stresses the need to forecast specific goals and eliminates the need to focus on tasks needed to accomplish goals
    C. may illustrate duplication of effort between interdependent activities
    D. shows the relationship between various organizational segments

25. A line-item budget is a GOOD control budget because

    A. it clearly specifies how the items being purchased will be used
    B. expenditures can be shown primarily for contractual services
    C. it clearly specifies what the money is buying
    D. it clearly specifies the services to be provide

KEY (CORRECT ANSWERS)

1. C	11. D
2. C	12. D
3. C	13. A
4. D	14. B
5. A	15. C
6. A	16. A
7. B	17. A
8. B	18. D
9. D	19. A
10. D	20. C

21. B
22. D
23. B
24. B
25. C

EXAMINATION SECTION
TEST 1

DIRECTIONS: Each question or incomplete statement is followed by several suggested answers or completions. Select the one that BEST answers the question or completes the statement. *PRINT THE LETTER OF THE CORRECT ANSWER IN THE SPACE AT THE RIGHT.*

1. A _____ is a grant made by a nonprofit with funds it has raised specifically for making a grant.
    A. regrant
    B. renewal grant
    C. matching grant
    D. corporate sponsorship

1.____

2. When narrowing your prospect list, you should try to limit it to no more than _____ prospects whose funding priorities closely match your mission.
    A. 100   B. 50   C. 25   D. 10

2.____

3. _____ was the first website to make 990 forms available for all non-profits.
    A. Foundation Center
    B. GuideStar
    C. Grants.gov
    D. GrantStation

3.____

4. Most private and corporate foundations will allow an indirect expense in your project of _____ without questioning it or requiring documentation.
    A. 20-30%
    B. 15-20%
    C. 5-15%
    D. less than 50%

4.____

5. What are the two types of federal grants?
    A. Formula grants and project grants
    B. Process grants and objective grants
    C. Private grants and public grants
    D. RFPs and contracts

5.____

6. A corporate sponsorship proposal differs from a grant proposal and focuses on
    A. program details
    B. organization history
    C. long-term objectives
    D. constituent demographics

6.____

7. All of the following information can be found in a 990-PF EXCEPT
    A. a foundation's needs statement
    B. whether or not a foundation received contributions during the year
    C. a complete list of foundation trustees
    D. salaries of top level foundation staff

7.____

8. A primary feature of a _____ foundation is that it consists of several funds, each created by a different donor seeking to enhance one aspect of life in a specific community.
   A. charitable trust
   B. community
   C. corporate
   D. family

8._____

9. In a _____ foundation, most if not all of the trustees are related to the foundation's founder.
   A. family
   B. community
   C. government
   D. corporate

9._____

10. A challenge grant that requires you to match the grant equally is considered a _____ match.
    A. two to one
    B. three to one
    C. one to one
    D. two to three

10._____

11. If you organize a grant proposal using the _____ method, you focus on the results anticipated at the end of the program.
    A. outcomes
    B. process
    C. need-based
    D. metric

11._____

12. _____ is revenue not dependent on grants that can come from service fees, product sales or other non-grant sources.
    A. Earned income
    B. Discretionary sponsorship
    C. Formula grant revenue
    D. Operating support

12._____

13. Grants awarded on merit rather than financial need are known as _____ grants.
    A. formula
    B. discretionary
    C. challenge
    D. competitive

13._____

14. The trustee of a private foundation has designed a grant that lies outside the foundation's guidelines. This is an example of a _____ grant.
    A. formula
    B. discretionary
    C. challenge
    D. competitive

14._____

15. Terrence is a freelance grant writer who wants to review federal grant RFPs. Where should he look?

    A. Grants.gov
    B. The Foundation Center website
    C. GrantStation.com
    D. The Donor's Forum website

16. _____ grants are larger grants given to local governments by the federal government so they can redistribute the grants locally.

    A. Community development block
    B. Discretionary
    C. Intermediary
    D. Multi-year

17. Which of the following is required in all federal grant applications?

    A. 509(a) designation
    B. An EIN
    C. DUNS number
    D. Demonstration of corporate sponsorship

18. _____ foundations, which are usually established by one or two donors, are the largest group of private foundations.

    A. Local
    B. Federal
    C. Corporate
    D. Family

19. What is the primary difference between a private independent foundation and a family foundation?

    A. Amount of grants distributed
    B. Types of projects funded
    C. Composition of the board
    D. Required tax designation

20. Which type of foundation makes almost 90% of all grants made by foundations annually?

    A. Private   B. Corporate   C. Federal   D. State

21. Which of the following features separates a community foundation from family, private independent and most corporate foundations?

    A. A community foundation does not raise funds
    B. A community foundation only makes grants to large, well-established organizations
    C. A community foundation has a board constructed of family members of the founder
    D. A community foundation both raises funds and makes grants

22. You should never apply for a grant from a _____ foundation that is in a different geographic region or city than your non-profit organization.
    A. corporate
    B. community
    C. private independent
    D. family

22._____

23. What IRS designation categorizes an organization as either a public charity or a private foundation?
    A. 509(a)
    B. 990-PF
    C. 1040-A
    D. 950(b)

23._____

24. The federal government requires grant applicants to sign and submit forms stating that the organization practices equal opportunity, has an environmental policy or agrees to some other requirement. These are known as _____.
    A. bylaws
    B. assurances
    C. abstracts
    D. checklists

24._____

25. A wealthy donor has endowed money to a private foundation so the foundation can provide money to non-profit agencies that serve the community. This money is known as
    A. an excise
    B. leverage
    C. a corpus
    D. a payout requirement

25._____

KEY (CORRECT ANSWERS)

1. A
2. D
3. B
4. C
5. A

6. D
7. A
8. B
9. A
10. C

11. A
12. A
13. D
14. B
15. A

16. A
17. C
18. D
19. C
20. A

21. D
22. B
23. A
24. B
25. C

TEST 2

DIRECTIONS: Each question or incomplete statement is followed by several suggested answers or completions. Select the one that BEST answers the question or completes the statement. *PRINT THE LETTER OF THE CORRECT ANSWER IN THE SPACE AT THE RIGHT.*

1. What minimum legal requirement must an organization meet in order to receive grants?
    A. It must have 501(c)(3) tax-exempt nonprofit status
    B. It must publically release a 990-PF statement
    C. It must be in operation for at least two years
    D. It must operate with a budgetary surplus for at least one year

    1._____

2. What is one benefit of challenge grants?
    A. They are reserved only for new organizations or new programs and are therefore less competitive
    B. They do not have as many restrictions and require less paperwork
    C. They tend to have a broader community impact than other grants
    D. Every dollar raised is used to bring in more money

    2._____

3. Solicited projects are usually initiated through
    A. an applicant's grant proposal
    B. Requests for Proposals (RFPs) and program announcements
    C. the submission of 990-PF forms
    D. program announcements and annual reports

    3._____

4. In project management, a(n) _____ is a starting point used to measure or compare a project's progress.
    A. endowment
    B. asset
    C. baseline
    D. donee

    4._____

5. For the most part, organizations raise funds for general operating support
    A. from individuals, through annual appeals
    B. from corporate foundations
    C. through seed grants
    D. through capital campaigns

    5._____

6. Generally, foundations tend to prefer providing funding for _____ rather than _____.
    A. start-ups; established organizations
    B. general operating support; projects
    C. faith-based organizations; secular organizations
    D. projects; general operating support

    6._____

7. A nonprofit organization is dedicated to providing fresh, local food to people in New York City. In order to fulfill his organization's mission, the executive director wants to purchase a vacant lot and convert it to a community garden. Because he wants to purchase a new piece of property, this is an example of a(n) _____ expense.
     A. in-kind
     B. capital
     C. matching
     D. endowment

8. What types of organizations usually seek endowment funding?
     A. Start-up organizations
     B. Organizations with a large financial deficit
     C. Well-established organizations
     D. Organizations looking to purchase a new building

9. When an organization offers operational or management assistance with fundraising, budgeting, financial planning, program planning or other specialized tasks, it is providing
     A. technical assistance
     B. matching funds
     C. capital support
     D. program-related investment

10. A(n) _____ is the minimum amount private foundations are required to expend for charitable purposes.
     A. asset deduction
     B. program-related investment
     C. qualifying distribution
     D. payout requirement

Questions 11-15

DIRECTIONS: In questions 11 through 15, match the grant proposal component in Column A to its correct location within a foundation grant proposal in Column B.

Column A	Column B
11. Executive summary	A. First
12. Statement of need	B. Second
13. Project description	C. Third
14. Attachments	D. Fourth
15. Title page	E. Last

16. How do community foundations differ from other types of public foundations? 16._____
    A. They are owned by corporations
    B. They have different grantmaking priorities
    C. They do not have to file a 990-PF
    D. They have a board of directors

17. Which of the following is TRUE of government funding? 17._____
    A. Government funding is less competitive than other types of nonprofit funding
    B. Government grant awards usually require that you pay them back
    C. Government funding is only provided for solicited project ideas
    D. Federal government funders usually prefer projects that can act as prototypes and be replicated by other organizations

18. Marty is performing research on a corporate foundation that he thinks might be a good funding match for his organization. He's already looked at the foundation's profile on the Foundation Center's website. What else should he do in his research? 18._____
    A. Call the corporation and ask to speak to the CEO.
    B. Send a letter of inquiry to the foundation and see if he gets a response
    C. Look at the corporation's website
    D. Call the foundation and ask to speak to someone on the board of directors

19. Which of the following is NOT a way to access a copy of a foundation's 990-PF? 19._____
    A. Request it from the IRS
    B. Look it up on guidestar.org
    C. Request it from the nonprofit organization itself
    D. Request it from your local public records office

20. When a private foundation makes a grant to an organization that is not classified by the IRS as a "public charity," the grant is known as a(n) _____ grant. 20._____
    A. endowment
    B. expenditure responsibility
    C. in-kind
    D. matching

21. A nonprofit organization has just been awarded a multi-year grant that becomes smaller each year with the expectation that the organization will gradually begin to increase its fundraising from other sources. This is known as a(n) _____ grant. 21._____
    A. cooperative
    B. in-kind
    C. declining
    D. demonstration

22. Certain foundations use the majority of their income to fund charitable programs of their own, and make very few grants to outside organizations. These are known as _____ foundations. 22._____
    A. operating   B. public   C. corporate   D. grassroots

23. What type of grant evaluation reviews the outcome of a grant in order to determine whether or not the grant achieved its primary objective?   23._____
    A. Outside
    B. Post-grant
    C. Inside
    D. Short-term

24. A letter of inquiry is also often referred to as a letter of intent or a(n) _____.   24._____
    A. endowment
    B. giving circle
    C. annual report
    D. preliminary proposal

25. A worker at a homeless shelter is preparing for a meeting with a board member from a foundation that has contributed generously to the shelter in the past year. The board member is coming to see the shelter in person, meet the staff and talk to some recipients of the shelter's services.   25._____
    This is known as a(n)_____.
    A. site visit
    B. feasibility study
    C. annual report
    D. bequest

KEY (CORRECT ANSWERS)

1. A   11. B
2. D   12. C
3. B   13. D
4. C   14. E
5. A   15. A

6. D   16. B
7. B   17. D
8. C   18. C
9. A   19. D
10. D   20. B

21. C
22. A
23. B
24. D
25. A

EXAMINATION SECTION
TEST 1

DIRECTIONS: Each question or incomplete statement is followed by several suggested answers or completions. Select the one that BEST answers the question or completes the statement. *PRINT THE LETTER OF THE CORRECT ANSWER IN THE SPACE AT THE RIGHT.*

1. A(n) _____ grant provides funding to achieve a specific outcome during an established period of time.
    A. operating
    B. external
    C. RFP
    D. project

    1._____

2. A worker at a local animal shelter has devised an idea for a project that rehabilitates abused animals. She would like to acquire funding for her project and has submitted grant proposals to numerous funders. Since she is seeking funding for a project she created herself, it would be considered a(n) _____ project idea.
    A. unsolicited
    B. solicited
    C. endowment
    D. operating

    2._____

3. Which of the following is an example of a public funding source?
    A. Foundations
    B. Corporations
    C. Federal government
    D. Special interest groups

    3._____

4. Which of the following is NOT an example of an in-kind contribution?
    A. Financial award used to purchase new computers for a school
    B. A company's donation of used computers to a school
    C. Print shop offering to print all of a nonprofit's program materials for free
    D. Graphic designer offering to design all of a nonprofit's program materials for free

    4._____

5. Which document provides important financial information about a private foundation including a list of all their grantees, their giving interests, restrictions, application procedures and deadlines?
    A. 1040-A
    B. 990-PF
    C. Form 1120
    D. W-9

    5._____

23

6. Most grantmakers require _____ before they allow applicants to submit a full grant proposal.
   A. a letter of recommendation
   B. a face-to-face meeting
   C. submission of a 990-PF
   D. a letter of inquiry

   6._____

7. Which of the following is NOT a major component of a grant proposal to state and federal agencies?
   A. Statement of purpose
   B. Statement of need
   C. An RFP
   D. Signed assurances

   7._____

8. Unless guidelines specify that it is not necessary, nonprofits should always attach _____ to grant proposals.
   A. their 501(c)(3) letter
   B. their 990-PF form
   C. an RFP
   D. a letter of inquiry

   8._____

9. Although the _____ is usually one of the first items in a grant proposal, it is often written last because it requires that all aspects of the proposal be clearly defined.
   A. statement of need
   B. executive summary
   C. statement of purpose
   D. qualifications/personnel section

   9._____

10. Generally, purpose statements in well-crafted grant proposals include which of the following three components?
    A. Goals, objectives and outcomes
    B. Goals, outcomes and externalities
    C. Qualifications, goals and objectives
    D. Targets, benchmarks and externalities

    10._____

Questions 11-15

DIRECTIONS: In questions 11 through 15, match the grant type in Column A to its description in Column B.

Column A	Column B	
11. Operating grant	A. funds used to build or remodel facilities	11._____
12. Start-up award	B. monies matched by applicant or another source	12._____
13. Challenge grant	C. general financial support to an organization	13._____
14. Capital award	D. funds to be invested and the interest spent	14._____
15. Endowment grant	E. funds to help an organization begin an initiative	15._____

16. What is the difference between indirect and direct costs?
    A. Direct costs are specifically related to the project, whereas indirect costs relate to the infrastructure necessary to support the project
    B. Direct costs are tax-deductible, whereas indirect costs are not
    C. Indirect costs are specifically related to the project, whereas direct costs relate to the infrastructure necessary to support the project
    D. Indirect costs are tax-deductible, whereas direct costs are not

17. Which of the following is usually considered an indirect cost?
    A. A project manager's salary
    B. Printing costs for a publication announcing a project to the community
    C. A project manager's travel expenses
    D. An organization's rent

18. Project staff salaries and benefits should be included under which budget category?
    A. Other expenses
    B. Personnel
    C. Indirect costs
    D. Overhead expenses

19. Some grant proposal applications will request a(n) _____, in which the organization can explain in writing its reasoning for its financial decisions.
    A. statement of purpose
    B. in-kind budget
    C. budget narrative
    D. operating budget

20. Which type of evaluation provides information that is useful while a program is being implemented?
    A. Formative
    B. Summative
    C. Impact
    D. Outcome

21. Which of the following should NOT be included in the "Procedures" section of a grant proposal?
    A. Deliverables
    B. Accomplishments to date
    C. A plan for dissemination
    D. The budget

22. If a grantmaker asks an organization to specify the amount of homeless people who will receive temporary housing as a result of its program, the grantmaker is interested in _____.
    A. outcomes
    B. outputs
    C. procedures
    D. inputs

23. Which of the following is an example of a behavioral objective statement?

   A. Twenty of 40 participants will learn how to use mnemonic devices to improve their memory retention.
   B. Increase the reading comprehension of ESL students at Cross Community College.
   C. Program staff will develop two reading comprehension protocols in the first month and will use evaluation to determine which is most effective.
   D. Within two months, all participants will pass a skills test demonstrating their ability to read at the high-school level.

24. A(n) _____ is a general description of what you want a project to accomplish.

   A. benchmark statement
   B. thesis
   C. goal statement
   D. objective statement

25. In a grant proposal, an abstract can also be called a(n) _____.

   A. purpose statement
   B. statement of need
   C. benchmark statement
   D. executive summary

KEY (CORRECT ANSWERS)

1. D	11. C
2. A	12. E
3. C	13. B
4. A	14. A
5. B	15. D
6. D	16. A
7. C	17. D
8. A	18. B
9. B	19. C
10. A	20. A

21. D
22. B
23. A
24. C
25. D

TEST 2

DIRECTIONS: Each question or incomplete statement is followed by several suggested answers or completions. Select the one that BEST answers the question or completes the statement. *PRINT THE LETTER OF THE CORRECT ANSWER IN THE SPACE AT THE RIGHT.*

1. Foundations typically have _____, or fields of interest in which they are more likely to grant funds.
    A. funding priorities
    B. externalities
    C. case histories
    D. project initiatives

    1._____

2. Which type of organization exists solely to make charitable contributions that benefit a specific community or region?
    A. Company-sponsored foundation
    B. Cooperative venture
    C. Federated giving program
    D. Community foundation

    2._____

3. Which of the following is NOT one of the three types of private foundations?
    A. Independent
    B. Governmental
    C. Corporate
    D. Operating

    3._____

4. Which of the following is an example of a federated giving program?
    A. National Endowment for the Arts
    B. Koch Family Foundation
    C. United Way
    D. Environmental Protection Agency

    4._____

5. Which component of a grant proposal explains why the project is necessary?
    A. Statement of need
    B. Conclusion
    C. Budget
    D. Project description

    5._____

6. An individual on the board of a foundation who helps decide what projects and organizations the foundation will fund is a(n) _____.
    A. program manager
    B. executive director
    C. trustee
    D. donee

    6._____

7. Which of the following should NOT be included in a Letter of Inquiry?
    A. Name and mission of your organization
    B. Amount requested and what it will cover
    C. Brief statement of the problem or need
    D. Budget narrative

8. Which of the following sections of a grant proposal is typically the longest?
    A. Project description
    B. Conclusion
    C. Budget
    D. Executive summary

9. The _____ in a grant proposal should consist of about two paragraphs that summarize the proposal's main points.
    A. statement of need
    B. conclusion
    C. budget
    D. qualifications/personnel section

10. A private foundation that only awards grants in a few or less-interest areas is a
    A. general purpose foundation
    B. special purpose foundation
    C. federated giving program
    D. funding information network

Questions 11-15

DIRECTIONS: For questions 11 through 15, match the grant proposal component in Column A to its function in Column B.

Column A

11. Executive summary
12. Statement of need
13. Project description
14. Budget
15. Organization information

Column B

A. outlines the financial details of the project
B. provides information about the nonprofit applying
C. explains the steps in project implementation
D. presents the case and summarizes the proposal
E. describes why the project is necessary

16. Which of the following is an example of a benchmark outcome statement?
    A. Increase by 30 percent all 9th graders' algebra skills in Thomas Jefferson High School compared to their scores on standardized tests in 2013
    B. Increase math skills of all 9th grade students in Thomas Jefferson High School
    C. Increase the number of 9th grade students with grade-appropriate math skills
    D. Increase by 30 percent all 9th graders' algebra skills in Thomas Jefferson High School

17. A(n) _____ statement outlines a precise and measurable consequence of a project. 17._____

    A. goal
    B. objective
    C. abstract
    D. unsolicited

18. What is the difference between a grant and a contract? 18._____

    A. Nothing; they are one in the same.
    B. Contracts are usually awarded through an RFP in which the funder has already outlined the details and parameters of the project, whereas grants are usually awarded for projects in which the nonprofit has developed the project details and presented it to the funder
    C. Grants are awarded by private foundations, whereas contracts are awarded by corporate foundations
    D. Grants are usually awarded through an RFP in which the funder has already outlined the details and parameters of the project, whereas contracts are usually awarded for projects in which the nonprofit has developed the project details and presented it to the funder

19. A 501(c)(3) form is required with nearly every grant proposal because it 19._____

    A. demonstrates an organization's longevity
    B. demonstrates an organizations fiscal sustainability
    C. proves that an organization is publically traded
    D. proves an organization's nonprofit status

20. What is the difference between a corporate foundation and a corporate giving program? 20._____

    A. Corporate foundations are separate legal entities from their parent corporation, are tax-exempt, and are therefore subject to certain disclosure requirements, whereas corporate giving programs are not separate legal entities from their parent company and are thus not subject to the same disclosure requirements
    B. Nothing; they are one in the same
    C. Corporate foundations are private, general purpose foundations, whereas corporate giving programs are public, special purpose foundations
    D. Corporate giving programs are separate legal entities from their parent corporation, are tax-exempt, and are therefore subject to certain disclosure requirements, whereas corporate foundations are not separate legal entities from their parent company and are thus not subject to the same disclosure requirements

21. Kara is writing a grant proposal to secure funding for the inner-city after-school reading program she runs. Which of the following people would be internal stakeholder(s) for Kara's program?
    A. Principals of local schools she collaborates with
    B. Parents of the students who participate
    C. Students who participate
    D. The program manager

22. A(n) _____ is a document voluntarily issued by a foundation or corporation that includes its financial information and outlines its grant making activities.
    A. 990-PF
    B. distribution letter
    C. annual report
    D. grantee financial report

23. A grant writer for an organization called Organic Consumers Unite has recently been awarded a grant from the Valerie P. Murdock Foundation. In this example, Organic Consumers Unite is the _____ and the Valerie P. Murdock Foundation is the _____.
    A. trustee; donor
    B. donee; donor
    C. trustee; donee
    D. donor; donee

24. If two or more grantmakers share funding responsibilities or contribute information or resources to the same project, it is known as a _____.
    A. corporate giving program
    B. federated giving program
    C. cooperative venture
    D. community fund

25. Olive works for an office supply company, and the company has offered to match dollar-for-dollar any donation Olive makes to a charitable organization of her choice. This is known as a(n) _____.
    A. employee-matching grant
    B. endowment
    C. benchmark grant
    D. cooperative venture

KEY (CORRECT ANSWERS)

1. A
2. D
3. B
4. C
5. A

6. C
7. D
8. A
9. B
10. B

11. D
12. E
13. C
14. A
15. B

16. A
17. B
18. B
19. D
20. A

21. D
22. C
23. B
24. C
25. A

EXAMINATION SECTION

TEST 1

DIRECTIONS: Each question or incomplete statement is followed by several suggested answers or completions. Select the one that BEST answers the question or completes the statement. *PRINT THE LETTER OF THE CORRECT ANSWER IN THE SPACE AT THE RIGHT.*

Question 1 refers to the following passage:

Competition and the resulting race for higher productivity and new markets had costs as well as benefits. New technology demanded that factories operate at near-capacity in order to produce goods most economically. Because of this:
- The more manufacturers produced, the more they had to sell
- To sell more, they had to reduce prices
- To profit more, they expanded further and often reduced wages
- To expand, they had to borrow money
- To repay the money, they had to produce and sell even more

1. Which of the following best describes how U.S. business leaders attempted to deal with the dilemma described in the passage?
    A. They formed large enterprises that merged the assets of major competitors in an industry
    B. They developed more cooperative ways to deal with organized labor
    C. They made extensive use of the scientific management principles of Frederick Winslow Taylor
    D. They tried to increase exports by calling for the elimination of protective tariffs

1._____

2. Which of the following is the most accurate comparison of the two companies represented in the organizational charts below?

2._____

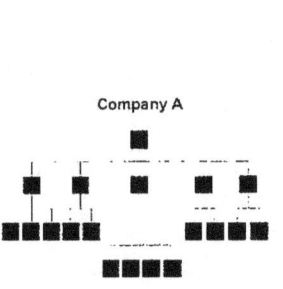
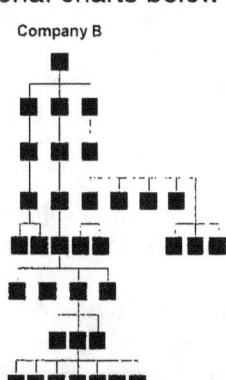

   A. The work force in Company B has considerably higher skill levels than the work force in Company A
   B. Company B is more likely than Company A to experience delays in the flow of information
   C. Lower-level managers in Company B have more decision-making authority than lower-level managers in Company A
   D. Company B is better able than Company A to adjust to unexpected changes in business conditions

3. Human resource managers can best ensure high job performance and work satisfaction among employees by
   A. basing employee compensation on current market standards
   B. putting all new employees through a comprehensive orientation process
   C. devising objective measures of employee performance
   D. developing procedures to match the right person to the right job

   3._____

4. Which of the following best describes an important difference between partnerships and the corporate form of business organization?
   A. Transfer of ownership has limited effect on the status of a partnership
   B. The liability of corporate owners is limited to the amount of stock they own
   C. The life of a partnership is unlimited
   D. Corporations do not have to pay state income taxes on their profits

   4._____

5. A researcher would be best advised to use a stratified sample for a marketing survey when there is a strong likelihood that
   A. factors such as age and gender will influence the answers of respondents
   B. respondents will not provide accurate answers to certain types of questions
   C. low response rates will distort the representativeness of the sample
   D. factors such as survey complexity will prevent the timely collection of data

   5._____

6. Marketers should place particular emphasis on communicating the competitive advantages of a product when developing marketing strategies for which of the following types of commodities?
   A. Impulse products that consumers purchase without having planned to do so
   B. Attribute-based shopping products that consumers evaluate on the basis of product features before making a purchase
   C. Staples that are routinely purchased by consumers on a regular basis
   D. Specialty products for which consumers are willing to make special efforts to obtain preferred brands

   6._____

7. Which of the following types of promotions would be the most appropriate marketing objective for a product that has entered the maturity phase of the traditional product life cycle?
   A. Informative advertising designed to increase consumer awareness of the product's attributes
   B. Motivational advertising designed to generate enthusiasm for the product
   C. Competitive advertising designed to maintain a differential advantage over competing products
   D. Persuasive advertising designed to expand market distribution of the product

   7._____

8. To ensure that inventory is reordered at an appropriate time, it is most important that stores possess accurate information on which of the following?
    A. Per order processing costs and average monthly sales
    B. Total number of sales, slow-selling items and quantity discounts
    C. Order lead time, stock on hand and the usage rate
    D. Merchandise handling expenses and average inventory on hand

9. Which of the following best describes a major advantage and disadvantage of a specific advertising medium?
    A. Radio advertising enables firms to adopt a personal approach, but the per message cost is extremely high
    B. Although newspaper advertising offers a wide range of creative options, it has low credibility
    C. Direct mail advertising enables firms to target a specific audience, but there is a high throwaway rate
    D. Although magazine advertisements have a short lead time, they have low appeal to passive consumers

10. The owner of a delicatessen purchases four tables and a dozen chairs for $1,100, which will be paid in four quarterly installments during the next 12 months. Which of the following best describes the effect of this transaction on the business's accounts?
    A. Assets and owner equity increase by $1,100, and liabilities remain the same
    B. Assets, liabilities and owner equity all increase by $1,100
    C. Liabilities increase by $1,100, and assets and owner equity remain the same
    D. Both assets and liabilities increase by $1,100, and owner equity remains the same

11. Although the ToughSole Shoe Company's output and revenues have increased steadily in recent years, investors are worried about the high level of borrowing that has taken place to finance the firm's expansion. Changes in which of the following would most clearly reflect their concerns?
    A. Retained earnings
    B. Price-to-earnings ratio
    C. Dividend yield
    D. Debt-to-equity ratio

12. What amount should be recorded to retained earnings on this income statement? 12._____

```
            Worldwide Market Research, Inc.
                   Income Statement
            For month ending November 30, 20XX
         Services rendered        $11,100

         Revenues:
            Interest income           900

            Total Revenues                    $12,000

         Expenses:
            Equipment expense     $ 3,000
            Salaries expense        7,100

            Total expense                      10,100

         Net income before tax              $ 1,900

         Provision for income tax           $   310
```

   A. $1,590
   B. $2,210
   C. $10,410
   D. $12,310

13. Department A of Jones Retail has shown a net loss for the past two years, and company executives are thinking about eliminating the department. Based on information presented in the chart below, Jones Retail would be best advised to retain the department until its 13._____

	Avoidable Expenses	Unavoidable Expenses
Salaries of sales personnel	$ 30,000	
Advertising	3,000	
Supplies	800	
Depreciation, store equipment		$1,000
Rent		3,500
Insurance (merchandise and equipment)	1,400	400
Bad debts	400	
Share of general office expenses	600	3,800
Totals	$ 36,200	$8,700

   A. unavoidable expenses exceed $36,200
   B. annual loss exceeds $8,700
   C. avoidable share of general office expenses exceeds $3,800
   D. annual loss exceeds $36,200

14. A group discussion leader who is seeking to maximize interaction among individual group members would be best advised to adopt which of the seating arrangements shown below?

    I   II   III   IV

    A. I   B. II   C. III   D. IV

15. The arithmetic, logic and control circuits are elements of which of the following parts of a computer?
    A. Main memory
    B. Central processing unit (CPU)
    C. Disk drive
    D. Disk operating system (DOS)

16. An architectural firm would most likely use computer-assisted design (CAD) software for which of the following purposes?
    A. Create a marketing plan
    B. Evaluate alternative locations for a new building
    C. Develop a prototype of a new facility
    D. Analyze the work process in the drafting room

17. In which of the following situations would satellite telecommunications best be used?
    A. Broadcasting a local radio show
    B. Conducting a class through distance learning
    C. Making an analog telephone call
    D. Conducting a job interview

18. Password security on a network can best be maintained by adopting which of the following practices?
    A. Using passwords with an odd rather than even number of letters
    B. Using passwords that use a combination of letters and numbers
    C. Assigning the same password to entire departments of a company
    D. Having users enter a different password each time they log on

19. Which of the following would most likely cause the shift shown in the supply curve?   19._____

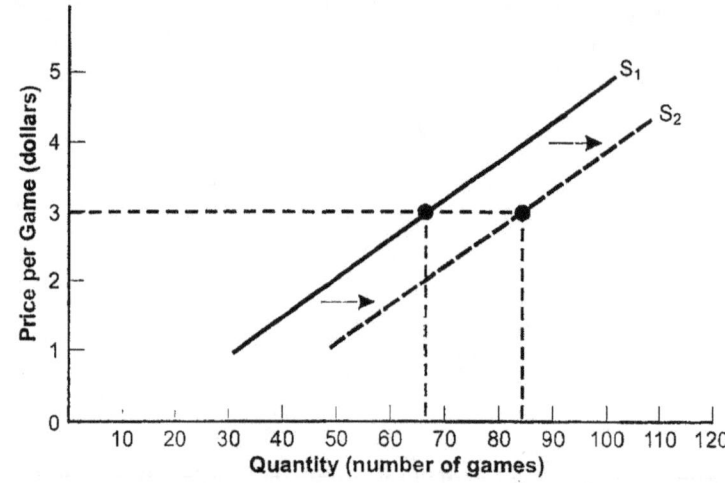

   A. Introduction of more efficient ways to manufacture and distribute games
   B. Increase in the labor costs of game producers
   C. Development of a popular alternative form of home entertainment
   D. Increase in the price of computer game players

20. Which characteristic of entrepreneurs most distinguishes them from other businesspeople?   20._____
   A. Their ability to combine resources to produce goods and services
   B. Their willingness to work long hours on a project
   C. Their ability to develop effective operating strategies for an enterprise
   D. Their willingness to take financial risks with their own capital

21. Which of the following best describes a major late-20th-century trend in international business history?   21._____
   A. Major industrial powers forged expansive new free-trade pacts that hindered the economic growth of developing countries
   B. Advances in communications technology created unprecedented opportunities for international trade
   C. Advances in manufacturing technology forced long-time opponents of free trade to abandon protectionist practices
   D. Disagreements about international labor standards prompted a resurgence of economic nationalism

22. Quality control workers at a ball-bearing plant inspect a random sample of output from company production lines each day. They are particularly concerned about any increase in the standard deviation of the bearings' diameter, as this would indicate that the   22._____
   A. bearings are larger than specified
   B. sample is too small for inspection purposes
   C. bearings are not perfectly smooth
   D. size of the bearings is inconsistent

23. Susan is uncertain whether to purchase collision coverage, an optional form of auto insurance that would pay for the repair or replacement of her car if she has an accident. Susan can best decide if it is advisable to obtain the additional coverage by determining
    A. what types of damage her car is likely to sustain in various types of accidents
    B. what it would cost to replace her car, compared to the cost of the coverage
    C. what the likelihood is that she will be in an accident during the life of the policy
    D. what her car cost when it was new, compared to the cost of the coverage

Use the list below of personal attitudes and attributes to answer question 24:

- Prefers varied duties to a familiar work routine
- Performs well under pressure
- Has superior written and verbal communication skills
- Is interested in pursuing opportunities for professional development
- Enjoys working with other people
- Is able to adapt quickly to unexpected developments

24. The attitudes and attributes listed above best match the personal characteristics needed for success in which of the following business career fields?
    A. Insurance and real estate
    B. Accounting
    C. Business data processing
    D. Public relations

KEY (CORRECT ANSWERS)

1. A	11. D	21. B
2. B	12. A	22. D
3. D	13. B	23. B
4. B	14. A	24. D
5. A	15. B	
6. B	16. C	
7. C	17. B	
8. C	18. B	
9. C	19. A	
10. D	20. D	

INTERPRETING STATISTICAL DATA
GRAPHS, CHARTS AND TABLES
EXAMINATION SECTION
TEST 1

DIRECTIONS: Each questioner incomplete statement is followed by several suggested answers or completions. Select the one that BEST answers the question or completes the statement. *PRINT THE LETTER OF THE CORRECT ANSWER IN THE SPACE AT THE RIGHT.*

Questions 1-3.

DIRECTIONS: Questions 1 through 3 are to be answered SOLELY on the basis of the following table.

QUARTERLY SALES REPORTED BY MAJOR INDUSTRY GROUPS

DECEMBER 2021 – FEBRUARY 2023
Reported Sales, Taxable & Non-Taxable (in Millions)

Industry Groups	12/21-2/22	3/22-5/22	6/22-8/22	9/22-11/22	12/22-2/23
Retailers	2,802	2,711	2,475	2,793	2,974
Wholesalers	2,404	2,237	2,269	2,485	2,974
Manufacturers	3,016	2,888	3,001	3,518	3,293
Services	1,034	1,065	984	1,132	1,092

1. The trend in total reported sales may be described as
   A. downward
   B. downward and upward
   C. horizontal
   D. upward

2. The two industry groups that reveal a similar seasonal pattern for the period December 2021 through November 2022 are

   A. retailers and manufacturers
   B. retailers and wholesalers
   C. wholesalers and manufacturers
   D. wholesalers and service

3. Reported sales were at a MINIMUM between

   A. December 2021 and February 2022
   B. March 2022 and May 2022
   C. June 2022 and August 2022
   D. September 2022 and November 2022

TEST 2

DIRECTIONS: Each question or incomplete statement is followed by several suggested answers or completions. Select the one that BEST answers the question or completes the statement. *PRINT THE LETTER OF THE CORRECT ANSWER IN THE SPACE AT THE RIGHT*

Questions 1-4.

DIRECTIONS: Questions 1 through 4 are to be answered SOLELY on the basis of the following information.

The income elasticity of demand for selected items of consumer demand in the United States are:

Item	Elasticity
Airline Travel	5.66
Alcohol	.62
Dentist Fees	1.00
Electric Utilities	3.00
Gasoline	1.29
Intercity Bus	1.89
Local Bus	1.41
Restaurant Meals	.75

1. The demand for the item listed below that would be MOST adversely affected by a decrease in income is

   A. alcohol
   B. electric utilities
   C. gasoline
   D. restaurant meals

2. The item whose relative change in demand would be the same as the relative change in income would be

   A. dentist fees
   B. gasoline
   C. restaurant meals
   D. none of the above

3. If income increases by 12 percent, the demand for restaurant meals may be expected to increase by

   A. 9 percent
   B. 12 percent
   C. 16 percent
   D. none of the above

4. On the basis of the above information, the item whose demand would be MOST adversely affected by an increase in the sales tax from 7 percent to 8 percent to be passed on to the consumer in the form of higher prices

   A. would be airline travel
   B. would be alcohol
   C. would be gasoline
   D. cannot be determined

TEST 3

DIRECTIONS: Each question or incomplete statement is followed by several suggested answers or completions. Select the one that BEST answers the question or completes the statement. *PRINT THE LETTER OF THE CORRECT ANSWER IN THE SPACE AT THE RIGHT.*

Questions 1-3.

DIRECTIONS: Questions 1 through 3 are to be answered SOLELY on the basis of the following graphs depicting various relationships in a single retail store.

GRAPH 1
RELATIONSHIP BETWEEN NUMBER OF CUSTOMERS STORE AND TIME OF DAY

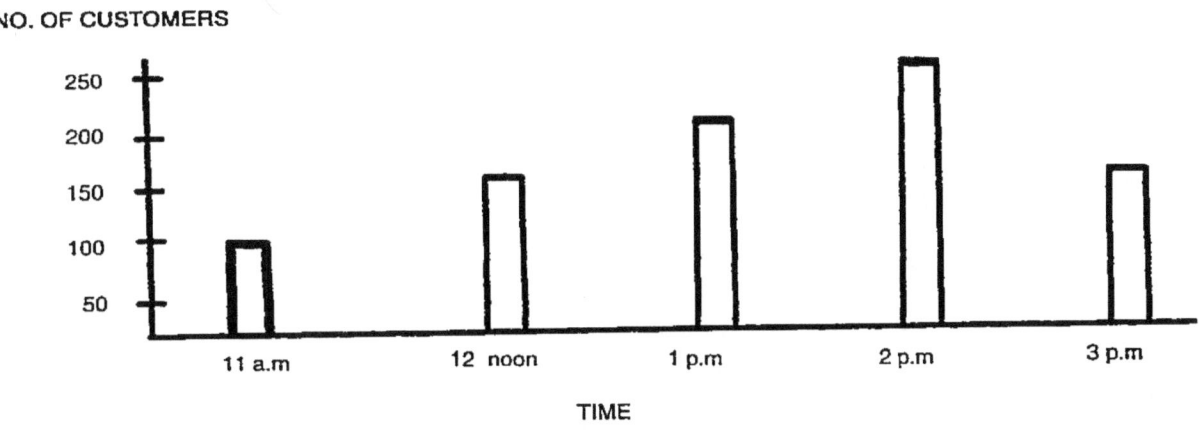

GRAPH II
RELATIONSHIP BETWEEN NUMBER OF CHECK-OUT LANES AVAILABLE IN STORE AND WAIT TIME FOR CHECK-OUT

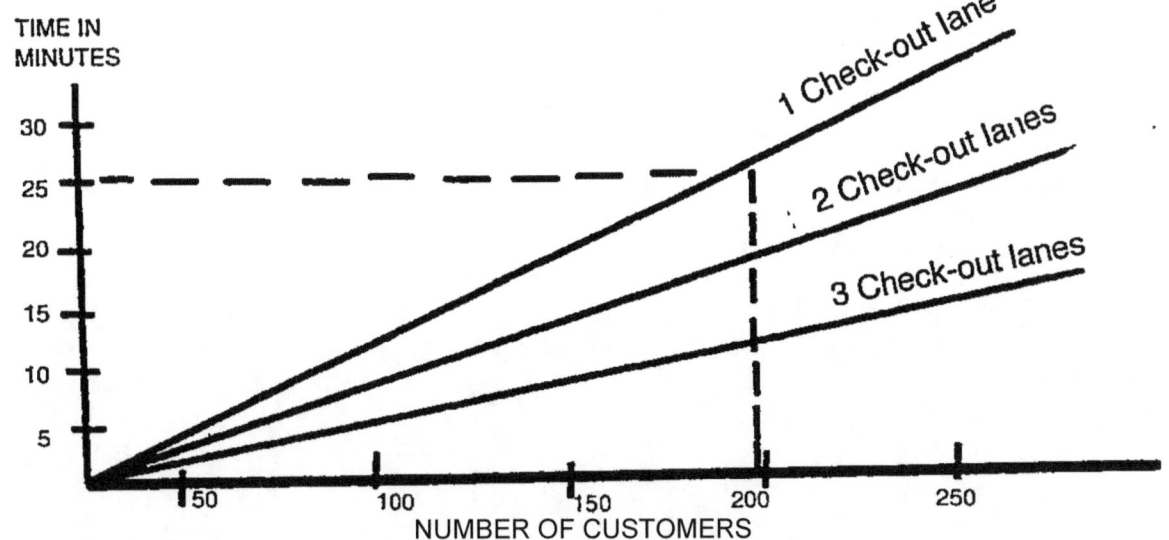

Note the dotted lines in Graph II. They demonstrate that, if there are 200 people in the store and only one check-out lane is open, the wait time will be 25 minutes.

43

1. At what time would a person be most likely NOT to have to wait more than 15 minutes if only one check-out lane is open?

   A. 11 A.M.   B. 12 Noon   C. 1 P.M.   D. 3 P.M.

2. At what time of day would a person have to wait the LONGEST to check out if three check-out lanes are available?

   A. 11 A.M.   B. 12 Noon   C. 1 P.M.   D. 2 P.M

3. The difference in wait times between 1 and 3 check-out lanes at 3 P.M. is MOST NEARLY

   A. 5   B. 10   C. 15   D. 20

TEST 4

DIRECTIONS: Each question or incomplete statement is followed by several suggested answers or completions. Select the one that BEST answers the question or completes the statement. *PRINT THE LETTER OF THE CORRECT ANSWER IN THE SPACE AT THE RIGHT.*

Questions 1-4.

DIRECTIONS: Questions 1 through 4 are to be answered SOLELY on the basis of the graph below.

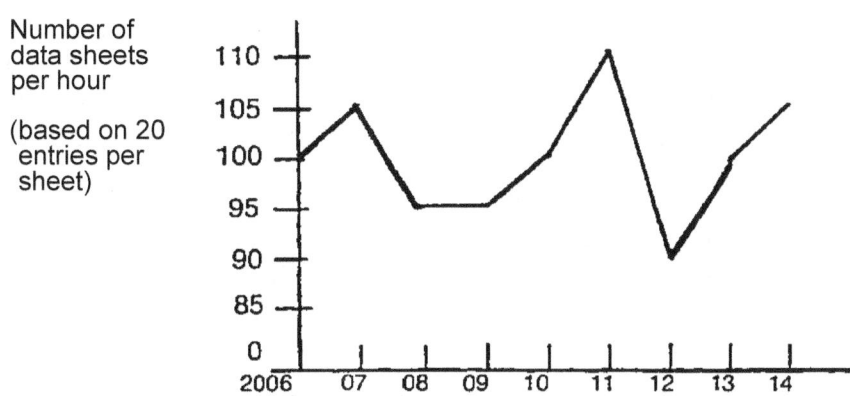

1. Of the following, during what four-year period did the average output of computer operators fall BELOW 100 sheets per hour?

    A. 2007-10   B. 2008-11   C. 2010-13   D. 2011-14

2. The average percentage change in output over the previous year's output for the years 2009 to 2012 is MOST NEARLY

    A. 2   B. 0   C. -5   D. -7

3. The difference between the actual output for 2012 and the projected figure based upon the average increase from 2006-2011 is MOST NEARLY

    A. 18   B. 20   C. 22   D. 24

4. Assume that after constructing the above graph you, an analyst, discovered that the average number of entries per sheet in 2012 was 25 (instead of 20) because of the complex nature of the work performed during that period.
The average output in sheets per hour for the period 2010-13, expressed in terms of 20 items per sheet, would then be MOST NEARLY

    A. 95   B. 100   C. 105   D. 110

TEST 6

DIRECTIONS: Each question or incomplete statement is followed by several suggested answers or completions. Select the one that BEST answers the question or completes the statement. *PRINT THE LETTER OF THE CORRECT ANSWER IN THE SPACE AT THE RIGHT.*

Questions 1-3.

DIRECTIONS: Questions 1 through 3 are to be answered on the basis of the following data assembled for a cost-benefit analysis.

	Cost	Benefit
No program	0	0
Alternative W	$ 3,000	$ 6,000
Alternative X	$10,000	$17,000
Alternative Y	$17,000	$25,000
Alternative Z	$30,000	$32,000

1. From the point of view of selecting the alternative with the best cost benefit ratio, the BEST alternative is Alternative

   A. W   B. X   C. Y   D. Z

2. From the point of view of selecting the alternative with the best measure of net benefit, the BEST alternative is Alternative

   A. W   B. X   C. Y   D. Z

3. From the point of view of pushing public expenditure to the point where marginal benefit equals or exceeds marginal cost, the BEST alternative is Alternative

   A. W   B. X   C. Y   D. Z

TEST 6

DIRECTIONS: Each question or incomplete statement is followed by several suggested answers or completions. Select the one that BEST answers the question or completes the statement. *PRINT THE LETTER OF THE CORRECT ANSWER IN THE SPACE AT THE RIGHT.*

Questions 1-3.

DIRECTIONS: Questions 1 through 3 are to be answered SOLELY on the basis of the following data.

A series of cost-benefit studies of various alternative health programs yields the following results:

Program	Benefit	Cost
K	30	15
L	60	60
M	300	150
N	600	500

In answering Questions 1 and 2, assume that all programs can be increased or decreased in scale without affecting their individual benefit-to-cost ratios.

1. The benefit-to-cost ratio of Program M is

    A. 10:1 B. 5:1 C. 2:1 D. 1:2

2. The budget ceiling for one or more of the programs included in the study is set at 75 units. It may MOST logically be concluded that

    A. Programs K and L should be chosen to fit within the budget ceiling
    B. Program K would be the most desirable one that could be afforded
    C. Program M should be chosen rather than Program K
    D. the choice should be between Programs M and K

3. If no assumptions can be made regarding the effects of change of scale, the MOST logical conclusion, on the basis of the data available, is that

    A. more data are needed for a budget choice of program
    B. Program K is the most preferable because of its low cost and good benefit-to-cost ratio
    C. Program M is the most preferable because of its high benefits and good benefit-to-cost ratio
    D. there is no difference between Programs K and M, and either can be chosen for any purpose

TEST 7

DIRECTIONS: Each question or incomplete statement is followed by several suggested answers or completions. Select the one that BEST answers the question or completes the statement. *PRINT THE LETTER OF THE CORRECT ANSWER IN THE SPACE AT THE RIGHT.*

Questions 1-6.

DIRECTIONS: Questions 1 through 6 are to be answered SOLELY on the basis of the information contained in the charts below which relate to the budget allocations of City X, a small suburban community. The charts depict the annual budget allocations by Department and by expenditures over a five-year period.

CITY X BUDGET IN MILLIONS OF DOLLARS
TABLE I. Budget Allocations by Department

Department	2017	2018	2019	2020	2021
Public Safety	30	45	50	40	50
Health and Welfare	50	75	90	60	70
Engineering	5	8	10	5	8
Human Resources	10	12	20	10	22
Conservation & Environment	10	15	20	20	15
Education & Development	15	25	35	15	15
TOTAL BUDGET	120	180	225	150	180

TABLE II. Budget Allocations by Expenditures

Category	2017	2018	2019	2020	2021
Raw Materials & Machinery	36	63	68	30	98
Capital Outlay	12	27	56	15	18
Personal Services	72	90	101	105	64
TOTAL BUDGET	120	180	225	150	180

1. The year in which the SMALLEST percentage of the total annual budget was allocated to the Department of Education and Development is

    A. 2017   B. 2018   C. 2020   D. 2021

2. Assume that in 2020 the Department of Conservation and Environment divided its annual budget into the three categories of expenditures and in exactly the same proportion as the budget shown in Table II for the year 2020. The amount allocated for capital outlay in the Department of Conservation and Environment's 2020 budget was MOST NEARLY _____ million.

    A. $2   B. $4   C. $6   D. $10

3. From the year 2018 to the year 2020, the sum of the annual budgets for the Departments of Public Safety and Engineering showed an overall _____ million.

   A. decline; $8
   B. increase; $7
   C. decline; $15
   D. increase; $22

4. The LARGEST dollar increase in departmental budget allocations from one year to the next was in _____ from _____.

   A. Public Safety; 2017 to 2018
   B. Health and Welfare; 2017 to 2018
   C. Education and Development; 2019 to 2020
   D. Human Resources; 2019 to 2020

5. During the five-year period, the annual budget of the Department of Human Resources was GREATER than the annual budget for the Department of Conservation and Environment in _____ of the years.

   A. none
   B. one
   C. two
   D. three

6. If the total City X budget increases at the same rate from 2021 to 2022 as it did from 2020 to 2021, the total City X budget for 2022 will be MOST NEARLY _____ million.

   A. $180
   B. $200
   C. $210
   D. $215

TEST 8

DIRECTIONS: Each question or incomplete statement is followed by several suggested answers or completions. Select the one that BEST answers the question or completes the statement. *PRINT THE LETTER OF THE CORRECT ANSWER IN THE SPACE AT THE RIGHT.*

Questions 1-3.

DIRECTIONS: Questions 1 through 3 are to be answered SOLELY on the basis of the following information.

Assume that in order to encourage Program A, the State and Federal governments have agreed to make the following reimbursements for money spent on Program A, provided the unreimbursed balance is paid from City funds.

During Fiscal Year 2021-2022 - For the first $2 million expended, 50% Federal reimbursement and 30% State reimbursement; for the next $3 million, 40% Federal reimbursement and 20% State reimbursement; for the next $5 million, 20% Federal reimbursement and 10% State reimbursement. Above $10 million expended, no Federal or State reimbursement.

During Fiscal Year 2022-2023 - For the first $1 million expended, 30% Federal reimbursement and 20% State reimbursement; for the next $4 million, 15% Federal reimbursement and 10% State reimbursement. Above $5 million expended, no Federal or State reimbursement.

1. Assume that the Program A expenditures are such that the State reimbursement for Fiscal Year 2021-2022 will be $1 million.
   Then, the Federal reimbursement for Fiscal Year 2021-2022 will be

   A. $1,600,000 B. $1,800,000
   C. $2,000,000 D. $2,600,000

2. Assume that $8 million were to be spent on Program A in Fiscal Year 2022-2023.
   The TOTAL amount of unreimbursed City funds required would be

   A. $3,500,000 B. $4,500,000
   C. $5,500,000 D. $6,500,000

3. Assume that the City desires to have a combined total of $6 million spent in Program A during both the Fiscal Year 2021-2022 and the Fiscal Year 2022-2023.
   Of the following expenditure combinations, the one which results in the GREATEST reimbursement of City funds is _____ in Fiscal Year 2021-2022 and _____ in Fiscal Year 2022-2023.

   A. $5 million; $1 million   B. $4 million; $2 million
   C. $3 million; $3 million   D. $2 million; $4 million

KEY (CORRECT ANSWERS)

TEST 1	**TEST 2**	**TEST 3**	**TEST 4**
1. D	1. B	1. A	1. A
2. C	2. A	2. D	2. B
3. C	3. A	3. B	3. C
	4. D		4. C

TEST 5	**TEST 6**	**TEST 7**	**TEST 8**
1. A	1. C	1. D	1. B
2. C	2. D	2. A	2. D
3. C	3. A	3. A	3. A
		4. B	
		5. B	
		6. D	

READING COMPREHENSION
UNDERSTANDING AND INTERPRETING WRITTEN MATERIAL
EXAMINATION SECTION
TEST 1

DIRECTIONS: Each question or incomplete statement is followed by several suggested answers or completions. Select the one that BEST answers the question or completes the statement. *PRINT THE LETTER OF THE CORRECT ANSWER IN THE SPACE AT THE RIGHT.*

1. The question *Who shall now teach Hegel?* is shorthand for the question *Who is going to teach this genre—all the so-called Continental philosophers?* The obvious answer to this question is *Whoever cares to study them.* This is also the right answer, but we can only accept it whole heartedly if we clear away a set of factitious questions. On such question is: *Are these Continental philosophers really philosophers?* Analytic philosophers, because they identify philosophical ability with argumentative skill and notice that there is nothing they would consider an argument in the bulk of Heidegger or Foucault, suggest that these must be people who tried to be philosophers and failed-incompetent philosophers. This is as silly as saying that Plato was an incompetent sophist, or that a hedgehog is an incompetent fox. Hegel knew what he thought about philosophers who imitated the method and style of mathematics. He thought they were incompetent. These reciprocal charges of incompetence do nobody any good. We should just drop the questions of what philosophy really is or who really counts as a philosopher.
Which sentence is BEST supported by the above paragraph?
   A. The study of Hegel's philosophy is less popular now than in the past.
   B. Philosophers must stop questioning the competence of other philosophers.
   C. Philosophers should try to be as tolerant as Foucault and Heidegger.
   D. Analytic philosophers tend to be more argumentative than other philosophers.

1.____

2. It is an interesting question: the ease with which organizations of different kinds at different stages in their history can continue to function with ineffectual leadership at the top, or even function without a clear system of authority. Certainly, the success of some experiments in worker self-management shows that bosses are not always necessary, as some contemporary Marxists argue. Indeed, sometimes the function of those at the top is merely to symbolize organizational accountability, especially in dealing with outside authorities, but not to guide the actions of those within the organization. A vice president of a large insurance company remarked to us that *Presidents are powerless; no one needs them. They should all be sent off to do public relations for the company.* While this is clearly a self-serving statement from someone next in line to command, it does give meaning to the expression being kicked upstairs. According to the author,

2.____

53

A. organizations function very smoothly without bosses
B. the function of those at the top is sometimes only to symbolize organizational accountability
C. company presidents are often inept at guiding the actions of those within the organization
D. presidents of companies have less power than one might assume they have

3. The goal of a problem is a terminal expression one wishes to cause to exist in the world of the problem. There are two types of goals: specified goal expressions in proof problems and incompletely specified goal expressions in find problems. For example, consider the problem of finding the value of X, given the expression 4X+5 = 17. In this problem, one can regard the goal expression as being of the form X = _____, the goal expression. The goal expression in a find problem of this type is incompletely specified. If the goal expression were specified completely—for example, X = 3—then the problem would be a proof problem, with only the sequence of operations to be determined in order to solve the problem. Of course, if one were not guaranteed that the goal expression X = 3 was true, then the terminal goal expression should really be considered to be incompletely specified—something like the statement X = 3 (true or false).
According to the preceding paragraph,
   A. the goal of the equation 4X+5 = 17 is true, not false
   B. if the goal expression was specified as being equal to 3, the problem 4X+5 = 17 would be a proof problem
   C. if the sequence of operations of the problem given in the paragraph is predetermined, the goal of the problem becomes one of terminal expression, or the number 17
   D. X cannot be found unless X is converted into a proof problem

3.____

4. We have human psychology and animal psychology, but no plant psychology. Why? Because we believe that plants have no perceptions or intentions. Some plants exhibit *behavior* and have been credited with *habits*. If you stroke the midrib of the compound leaf of a sensitive plant, the leaflets close. The sunflower changes with the diurnal changes in the source of light. The lowest animals have not much more complicated forms of behavior. The sea anemone traps and digests the small creatures that the water brings to it; the pitcher plant does the same thing and even more, for it presents a cup of liquid that attracts insects, instead of letting the surrounding medium drift them into its trap. Here as everywhere in nature where the great, general classes of living things diverge, the lines between them are not perfectly clear. A sponge is an animal; the pitcher plant is a flowering plant, but it comes nearer to *feeding itself* than the animal. Yet the fact is that we credit all animals, and only the animals, with some degree of feeling.
Of the following, the MAIN idea expressed in the above paragraph is:
   A. The classification of plants has been based on beliefs about their capacity to perceive and feel
   B. Many plants are more evolved than species considered animals

4.____

C. The lines that divide the classes of living things are never clear.
D. The abilities and qualities of plants are undervalued.

5. Quantitative indexes are not necessarily adequate measures of true economic significance or influence. But even the raw quantitative data speak loudly of the importance of the new transnationalized economy. The United Nations estimated value added in this new sector of the world economy at $500 billion in 2001, mounting to one-fifth of total GNP of the non-socialist world and exceeding the GNP of any one other country except the United States. Furthermore, all observers agree that the share of this sector in the world economy is growing rapidly. At least since 1980, its annual rate of growth has been high and remarkably steady at 10 percent compared to 4 percent for noninternationalized output in the Western developed countries.
One spokesman for the new system franklin envisages that within a generation some 400 to 500 multinational corporations will own close to two-thirds of the world's fixed assets.
According to the author, all of the following are true EXCEPT
   A. Quantitative indexes are not necessarily adequate measures of actual economic influence.
   B. The transnational sector of the world economy is growing rapidly.
   C. Since 1980, the rate of growth of transnationals has been 10% compared to 4% for internationalized output in the Western developed countries.
   D. Continued growth for multinational corporations is likely.

5.____

6. A bill may be sent to the Governor when it has passed both houses. During the session, he is given ten days to act on bills that reach his desk. Bills sent to him within ten days of the end of the session must be acted on within 30 days after the last day of the session. If the Governor takes no action on a ten day bill, it automatically becomes a law. If he disapproves or vetoes a ten day bill, it can become law only if it is re-passed by two-thirds vote in each house. If he fails to act on a 30 day bill, the bill is said to have received a *pocket veto*. It is customary for the Governor to act, however, on all bills submitted to him, and give his reason in writing for approving or disapproving important legislation.
According to the above paragraph, all of the following are true EXCEPT:
   A. Bills sent to the Governor in the last ten days of the session must be acted on within thirty days after the last day of the session,
   B. If the Governor takes no action on a 10 day bill, it is said to have received a *pocket veto*.
   C. It is customary for the Governor to act on all bills submitted to him.
   D. If the Governor vetoes a ten day bill, it can become law only if passed by a two-thirds vote of the Legislature.

6.____

7. It is particularly when I see a child going through the mechanical process of manipulating numbers without any intuitive sense of what it is all about that I recall the lines of Lewis Carroll: *Reeling and Writhing, of course, to begin with…and then the different branches of Arithmetic-Ambition, Distraction, Uglification, and Derision.* Or, as Max Beberman has put it, much more gently: *Somewhat related to the notion of discovery in teaching is our insistence that*

7.____

the student become aware of a concept before a name has been assigned to the concept. I am quite aware that the issue of intuitive understanding is a very live one among teachers of mathematics, and even a casual reading of the yearbook of the National Council of Teachers of Mathematics makes it clear that they are also very mindful of the gap that exists between proclaiming the importance of such understanding and actually producing it in the classroom.
The MAIN idea expressed in the above paragraph is:
   A. Math teachers are concerned about the difficulties inherent in producing an understanding of mathematics in their students.
   B. It is important that an intuitive sense in approaching math problems be developed, rather than relying on rote, mechanical learning.
   C. Mathematics, by its very nature, encourages rote, mechanical learning.
   D. Lewis Carroll was absolutely correct in his assessment of the true nature of mathematics.

8. Heisenberg's *Principle of Uncertainty*, which states that events at the atomic level cannot be observed with certainty, can be compared to this: In the world of everyday experience, we can observe any phenomenon and measure its properties without influencing the phenomenon in question to any significant extent. To be sure, if we try to measure the temperature of a demitasse with a bathtub thermometer, the instrument will absorb so much heat from the coffee that it will change the coffee's temperature substantially. But with a small chemical thermometer, we may get a sufficiently accurate reading. We can measure the temperature of a living cell with a miniature thermometer, which has almost negligible heat capacity. But in the atomic world, we can never overlook the disturbance caused by the introduction of the measuring apparatus.
Which sentence is BEST supported by the above paragraph?
   A. There is little we do not alter by the mere act of observation.
   B. It is always a good idea to use the smallest measuring device possible.
   C. Chemical thermometers are more accurate than bathtub thermometers.
   D. It is not possible to observe events at the atomic level and be sure that the same events would occur if we were not observing them.

9. It is a myth that American workers are pricing themselves out of the market, relative to workers in other industrialized countries of the world. The wages of American manufacturing workers increased at a slower rate in the 1990s than those of workers in other major western countries. In terms of American dollars, between 1990 and 2000, hourly compensation increased 489 percent in Japan and 464 percent in Germany, compared to 128 percent in the United States. Even though these countries experienced faster productivity growth, their unit labor costs still rose faster than in the United States, according to the Bureau of Labor Statistics. During the 1990s, unit labor costs rose 192 percent in Japan, 252 percent in Germany, and only 78 percent in the United States.
According to the above passage,
   A. unit labor costs in the 1990s were higher in Japan than they were in Germany or the United States
   B. the wages of American workers need to be increased to be consistent with other countries

C. American worker are more productive than Japanese or German workers
D. the wages of American workers in manufacturing increased at a slower rate in the 1990s than the wages of workers in Japan or Germany

10. No people have invented more ways to enjoy life than the Chinese, perhaps to balance floods, famines, warlords, and other ills of fate. The clang of gongs, clashing cymbals, and beating of drums sound through their long history. No month is without fairs and theatricals when streets are hung with fantasies of painted lanterns and crowded with *carriages that flow like water, horses like roaming dragons*. Night skies are illumined by firecrackers—a Chinese invention—bursting in the form of flowerpots, peonies, fiery devils. The ways of pleasure are myriad. Music plays in the air through bamboo whistles of different pitch tied to the wings of circling pigeons. To skim a frozen lake in an ice sleigh with a group of friends on a day when the sun is warm is rapture, like *moving in a cup of jade*. What more delightful than the ancient festival called *Half an Immortal*, when everyone from palace officials to the common man took a ride on a swing? When high in the air, one felt like an Immortal, when back to earth once again human—no more than to be for an instant a god.
    According to the above passage,
    A. if the Chinese hadn't had so many misfortunes, they wouldn't have created so many pleasurable past times
    B. the Chinese invented flowerpots
    C. every month the Chinese have fairs and theatricals
    D. pigeons are required to play the game *Half an Immortal*

10.____

11. In our century, instead, poor Diphilus is lost in the crowd of his peers. We flood one another. No one recognizes him as he loads his basket in the supermarket. What grevious fits of melancholy have I not suffered in one of our larger urban bookstores, gazing at the hundreds, thousands, tens of thousands of books on shelve and tables? And what are they to the hundreds of thousands, the millions that stand in our research libraries? More books than Noah saw raindrops. How many readers will read a given one of them—mine, yours—in their lifetimes? And how will it be in the distant future? Incomprehensible masses of books, Pelion upon Ossa, hordes of books, each piteously calling for attention, respect, love, in competition with the vast disgorgements of the past and with one another in the present. Neither is it at all helpful that books can even now be reduced to the size of a postage stamp. Avanti! Place the Bible on a pinhead! Crowding more books into small spaces does not cram more books into our heads. Here I come to the sticking point that unnerves the modern Diphilus. The number of books a person can read in a given time is, roughly speaking, a historical constant. It does not change significantly even when the number of books available for reading does. Constants are pitted against variables to confound both writer and reader.
    Of the following, the MAIN idea in this passage is:
    A. It is difficult to attain immortality because so many books are being published.
    B. Too many books are being published, so fewer people are reading them.

11.____

C. Because so many books are being published, the quality of the writing is poorer.
D. Because so many books are available, but only a fixed amount of time to read them, frustration results for both the reader and the writer.

12. Until recently, consciousness of sexual harassment has been low. But workers have become aware of it as more women have arrived at levels of authority in the workplace, feminist groups have focused attention on rape and other violence against women, and students have felt freer to report perceived abuse by professors. In the last 5 years, studies have shown that sexual misconduct at the workplace is a big problem. For example, in a recently published survey of federal employees, 42% of 694,000 women and 15% of 1,168,000 men said they had experienced some form of harassment. According to the author, 12.____
    A. the awareness of sexual harassment at the workplace is increasing
    B. the incidence of harassment is higher in universities than workplaces
    C. sexual harassment is much more commonly experienced by women than men
    D. it is rare for men to experience sexual harassment

Questions 13-17.

DIRECTIONS: Questions 13 through 17 are to be answered SOLELY on the basis of the following paragraph.

Since discounts are in common use in the commercial world and apply to purchases made by government agencies as well as business firms, it is essential that individuals in both public and private employment who prepare bills, check invoices, prepare payment vouchers, or write checks to pay bills have an understanding of the terms used. These include cash or time discount, trade discount, and discount series. A cash or time discount offers a reduction in price to the buyer for the prompt payment of the bill and is usually expressed as a percentage with a time requirement, stated in days, within which the bill must be paid in order to earn the discount. An example would be 3/10, meaning a 3% discount may be applied to the bill if the payment is forwarded to the vendor within 10 days. On an invoice, the cash discount terms are usually followed by the net terms, which is the time in days allowed for ordinary payment of the bill. Thus, 3/10, Net 30 means that full payment is expected in thirty days if the cash discount of 3% is not taken for having paid the bill within ten days. When the expression Terms Net Cash is listed on a bill, it means that no deduction for early payment is allowed. A trade discount is normally applied to list prices by a manufacturer to show the actual price to retailers so that they may know their cost and determine markups that will allow them to operate competitively and at a profit. A trade discount is applied by the seller to the list price and is independent of a cash or time discount. Discounts may also be used by manufacturers to adjust prices charged to retailers without changing list prices. This is usually done by series discounting and is expressed as a series of percentages. To compute a series discount, such as 40%, 20%, 10%, first apply the 40% discount to the list price, then apply the 20% discount to the remainder, and finally apply the 10% discount to the second remainder.

13. According to the above paragraph, trade discounts are
    A. applied by the buyer
    B. independent of cash discounts
    C. restricted to cash sales
    D. used to secure rapid payment of bills

14. According to the above paragraph, if the sales terms 5/10, Net 60 appear on a bill in the amount of $100 dated December 5 and the buyer submits his payment on December 15, his PROPER payment should be
    A. $60   B. $90   C. $95   D. $100

15. According to the above paragraph, if a manufacturer gives a trade discount of 40% for an item with a list price of $250 and the terms are Net Cash, the price a retail merchant is required to pay for this item is
    A. $250   B. $210   C. $150   D. $100

16. According to the above paragraph, a series discount of 25%, 20%, 10% applied to a list price of $200 results in an ACTUAL price to the buyer of
    A. $88   B. $90   C. $108   D. $110

17. According to the above paragraph, if a manufacturer gives a trade discount of 50% and the terms are 6/10, Net 30, the cost to a retail merchant of an item with a list price of $500 and for which he takes the time discount, is
    A. $220   B. $235   C. $240   D. $250

Questions 18-22.

DIRECTIONS: Questions 18 through 22 are to be answered SOLELY on the basis of the following paragraph.

The city may issue its own bonds or it may purchase bonds as an investment. Bonds may be issued in various denominations, and the face value of the bond is its par value. Before purchasing a bond, the investor desires to know the rate of income that the investment will yield. In computing the yield on a bond, it is assumed that the investor will keep the bond until the date of maturity, except for callable bonds which are not considered in this paragraph. To compute exact yield is a complicated mathematical problem, and scientifically prepared tables are generally used to avoid such computation. However, the approximate yield can be computed much more easily. In computing approximate yield, the accrued interest on the date of purchase should be ignored, because the buyer who pays accrued interest to the seller receives it again at the next interest date. Bonds bought at a premium (which cost more) yield a lower rate of income than the same bonds bought at par (face value), and bonds bought at a discount (which cost less) yield a higher rate of income than the same bonds bought at par.

18. An investor bought a $10,000 city bond paying 6% interest. Which of the following purchase prices would indicate that the bond was bought at a PREMIUM?
    A. $9,000   B. $9,400   C. $10,000   D. $10,600

19. During the year, a particular $10,000 bond paying 74% sold at fluctuating prices.
    Which of the following prices would indicate that the bond was bought at a DISCOUNT?
    A. $9,800   B. $10,000   C. $10,200   D. $10,750

20. A certain group of bonds was sold in denominations of $5,000, $10,000, $20,000 and $50,000.
    In the following list of four purchase prices, which one is MOST likely to represent a bond sold at par value?
    A. $10,500   B. $20,000   C. $22,000   D. $49,000

21. When computing the approximate yield on a bond, it is DESIRABLE to
    A. assume the bond was purchased at par
    B. consult scientifically prepared tables
    C. ignore accrued interest on the date of purchase
    D. wait until the bond reaches maturity

22. Which of the following is MOST likely to be an exception to the information provided in the above paragraph? Bonds
    A. purchased at a premium   B. sold at par
    C. sold before maturity   D. which are callable

Questions 23-25

DIRECTIONS: Questions 23 through 25 are to be answered SOLELY on the basis of the following paragraph.

There is one bad habit of drivers that often causes chain collisions at traffic lights. It is the habit of keeping one foot poised over the accelerator pedal, ready to step on the gas the instant the light turns green. A driver who is watching the light, instead of watching the cars in front of him, may *jump the gun* and bump the car in front of him, and this car in turn may bump the next car. If a driver is resting his foot on the accelerator, his foot will be slammed down when he bumps into the car ahead. This makes the collision worse and makes it very likely that cars further ahead in the line are going to get involved in a series of violent bumps.

23. Which of the following conclusions can MOST reasonably drawn from the information given in the above paragraph?
    A. American drivers have a great many bad driving habits.
    B. Drivers should step on the gas as soon as the light turns green.
    C. A driver with poor driving habits should be arrested and fined.
    D. A driver should not rest his foot on the accelerator when the car is stopped for a traffic light.

24. From the information given in the above paragraph, a reader should be able to tell that a chain collision may be defined as a collision
    A. caused by bad driving habits at traffic lights
    B. in which one car hits another, this second car hits a third car, and so on

C. caused by drivers who fail to use their accelerators
D. that takes place at an intersection where there is a traffic light

25. The above passage states that a driver who watches the light instead of paying attention to traffic may   25.____
    A. be involved in an accident   B. end up in jail
    C. lose his license   D. develop bad driving habits

KEY (CORRECT ANSWERS)

1. B
2. B
3. B
4. A
5. C

6. B
7. B
8. D
9. D
10. C

11. D
12. A
13. B
14. C
15. C

16. C
17. B
18. D
19. A
20. B

21. C
22. D
23. D
24. B
25. A

TEST 2

DIRECTIONS: Each question or incomplete statement is followed by several suggested answers or completions. Select the one that BEST answers the question or completes the statement. *PRINT THE LETTER OF THE CORRECT ANSWER IN THE SPACE AT THE RIGHT.*

Questions 1-4.

DIRECTIONS: Each of the statements in this section is followed by several labeled choices. In the space at the right, write the letter of the sentence which means MOST NEARLY what is stated or implied in the passage.

1. It may be said that the problem in adult education seems to be not the piling up of facts but practice in thinking.
   This statement means MOST NEARLY that
   A. educational methods for adults and young people should differ
   B. adults seem to think more than young people
   C. a well-educated adult is one who thinks but does not have a store of information
   D. adult education should stress ability to think

   1.____

2. Last year approximately 19,000 fatal accidents were sustained in industry. There were approximately 130 non-fatal injuries to each fatal injury.
   According to the above statement, the number of non-fatal accidents was
   A. 146,000   B. 190,000   C. 1,150,000   D. 2,500,000

   2.____

3. No employer expects his stenographer to be a walking encyclopedia, but it is not unreasonable for him to expect her to know where to look for necessary information on a variety of topics.
   The above statement means MOST NEARLY that the stenographer should
   A. be a college graduate
   B. be familiar with standard office reference books
   C. keep a scrapbook of all interesting happenings
   D. go to the library regularly

   3.____

4. For the United States, Canada has become the most important country in the world, yet there are few countries about which Americans know less. Canada is the third largest country in the world; only Russia and China are larger. The area of Canada is more than a quarter of the whole British Empire.
   According to the above statement, the
   A. British Empire is smaller than Russia or China
   B. territory of China is greater than that of Canada
   C. Americans know more about Canada than they do about China or Russia
   D. Canadian population is more than one-quarter the population of the British Empire

   4.____

Questions 5-8.

DIRECTIONS: Questions 5 through 8 are to be answered SOLELY on the basis of the following paragraph.

A few people who live in old tenements have had the bad habit of throwing garbage out of their windows, especially if there is an empty lot near their building. Sometimes the garbage is food; sometimes the garbage is half-empty soda cans. Sometimes the garbage is a little bit of both mixed together. These people just don't care about keeping the lot clean.

5. The above paragraph states that throwing garbage out of windows is a 5.____
   A. bad habit
   B. dangerous thing to do
   C. good thing to do
   D. good way to feed rats

6. According to the above paragraph, an empty lot next to an old tenement is sometimes used as a place to 6.____
   A. hold local gang meetings
   B. play ball
   C. throw garbage
   D. walk dogs

7. According to the above paragraph, which of the following throw garbage out of their windows? 7.____
   A. Nobody
   B. Everybody
   C. Most people
   D. Some people

8. According to the above paragraph, the kinds of garbage thrown out of windows are 8.____
   A. candy and cigarette butts
   B. food and half-empty soda cans
   C. fruit and vegetables
   D. rice and bread

Questions 9-12.

DIRECTIONS: Questions 9 through 12 are to be answered SOLELY on the basis of the following paragraph.

The game that is recognized all over the world as an all-American game is the game of baseball. As a matter of fact, baseball heroes like Joe DiMaggio, Willie Mays, and Babe Ruth were as famous in their day as movie stars Robert Redford, Paul Newman, and Clint Eastwood are now. All these men have had the experience of being mobbed by fans whenever they put in an appearance anywhere in the world. Such unusual popularity makes it possible for stars like these to earn at least as much money off the job as on the job. It didn't take manufacturers and advertising men long to discover that their sales of shaving lotion, for instance, increased when they got famous stars to advertise their product for them on radio and television.

9. According to the above paragraph, baseball is known everywhere as a(n) _____ game. 9.____
   A. all-American   B. fast   C. unusual   D. tough

10. According to the above paragraph, being so well known means that it is possible for people like Willie Mays and Babe Ruth to
    A. ask for anything and get it
    B. make as much money off the job as on it
    C. travel anywhere free of charge
    D. watch any game free of charge

10.____

11. According to the above paragraph, which of the following are known all over the world?
    A. Baseball heroes
    B. Advertising men
    C. Manufacturers
    D. Basketball heroes

11.____

12. According to the above paragraph, it is possible to sell much more shaving lotion on television and radio if
    A. the commercials are in color instead of black and white
    B. you can get a prize with each bottle of shaving lotion
    C. the shaving lotion makes you smell nicer than usual
    D. the shaving lotion is advertised by famous stars

12.____

Questions 13-15.

DIRECTIONS: Questions 13 through 15 are to be answered SOLELY on the basis of the following passage.

That music gives pleasure is axiomatic. Because this is so, the pleasures of music may seem a rather elementary subject for discussion. Yet the source of that pleasure, our musical instinct, is not at all elementary. It is, in fact, one of the prime puzzles of consciousness. Why is it that we are able to make sense out of these nerve signals so that we emerge from engulfment in the orderly presentation of sound stimuli as if we had lived through an image of life?

If music has impact for the mere listener, it follows that it will have much greater impact for those who sing it or play it themselves with proficiency. Any educated person in Elizabethan times was expected to read musical notation and take part in a madrigalsing. Passive listeners, numbered in the millions, are a comparatively recent innovation.

Everyone is aware that so-called serious music has made great strikes in general public acceptance in recent years, but the term itself still connotes something forbidding and hermetic to the mass audience. They attribute to the professional musician a kind of initiation into secrets that are forever hidden from the outsider. Nothing could be more misleading. We all listen to music, professionals, and non-professionals alike in the same sort of way, in a dumb sort of way, really, because simple or sophisticated music attracts all of us in the first instance, on the primordial level of sheer rhythmic and sonic appeal. Musicians are flattered, no doubt, by the deferential attitude of the layman in regard to what he imagines to be our secret understanding of music. But in all honesty, we musicians know that in the main we listen basically as others do, because music hits us with an immediacy that we recognize in the reactions of the most simple minded of music listeners.

13. A suitable title for the above passage would be   13.____
    A. HOW TO LISTEN TO MUSIC
    B. LEARNING MUSIC APPRECIATION
    C. THE PLEASURES OF MUSIC
    D. THE WORLD OF THE MUSICIAN

14. The author implies that the passive listener is one who   14.____
    A. cannot read or play music
    B. does not appreciate serious music
    C. does not keep time to the music by hand or toe tapping
    D. will not attend a concert if he has to pay for the privilege

15. The author of the above passage is apparently inconsistent when he discusses   15.____
    A. the distinction between the listener who pays for the privilege and the one who does not
    B. the historical development of musical forms
    C. the pleasures derived from music by the musician
    D. why it is that we listen to music

Questions 16-18.

DIRECTIONS: Questions 16 through 18 are to be answered SOLELY on the basis of the following passage.

Who are the clerisy? They are people who like to read books. The use of a word so unusual, so out of fashion, can only be excused on the ground that it has no familiar synonym. The word is little known because what it describes has disappeared, though I do not believe is gone forever. The clerisy are those who read for pleasure, but not for idleness; who read for pastime, but not to kill time; who love books, but do not live by books.

Let us consider the actual business of reading—the interpretive act of getting the words off the age and into your head in the most effective way. The most effective way is not the quickest way of reading; and for those who think that speed is the greatest good, there are plenty of manuals on how to read a book which profess to tell how to strip off the husk and guzzle the milk, like a chimp attacking a coconut. Who among today's readers would whisk through a poem, eyes aflicker, and say that he had read it? The answer to that last question must unfortunately be: far too many. For reading is not respected for the art it is.

Doubtless there are philosophical terms for the attitude of mind of which nasty reading is one manifestation, but here let us call it end-gaining, for its victims put ends before means; they value not reading, but having read. In this, the end-gainers make mischief and spoil all they do; end-gaining is one of the curses of our nervously tense, intellectually flabby civilization. In reading, as in all arts, it is the means, and not the end, which gives delight and brings the true reward. Not straining forward toward the completion, but the pleasure of every page as it comes, is the secret of reading. We must desire to read a book, rather than to have read it. This change in attitude, so simple to describe, is by no means simple to achieve,, if one has lived the life of an end-gainer.

16. A suitable title for the above passage would be
    A. READING FOR ENLIGHTENMENT
    B. THE ART OF RAPID READING
    C. THE WELL-EDUCATED READER
    D. VALUES IN READING

17. The author does NOT believe that most people read because they
    A. are bored
    B. have nothing better to do
    C. love books
    D. wish to say that they have read certain books

18. The change in attitude to which the author refers in the last sentence of the above passage implies a change from
    A. dawdling while reading so that the reader can read a greater number of books
    B. reading light fiction to reading serious fiction and non-fiction
    C. reading works which do not amuse the reader
    D. skimming through a book to reading it with care

Questions 19-22.

DIRECTIONS: Questions 19 through 22 are to be answered SOLELY on the basis of the following passage.

Violence is not new to literature. The writings of Shakespeare and Cervantes are full of it. But those classic writers did not condone violence. They viewed it as a just retribution for sins against the divine order or as a sacrifice sanctioned by heroism. What is peculiar to the modern literature is violence for the sake of violence. Perhaps our reverence for life has been dulled by mass slaughter, though mass slaughter has not been exceptional in the history of mankind. What is exceptional is the boredom that now alternates with war. The basic emotion in peacetime has become a horror of emptiness: a fear of being alone, of having nothing to do, a neurosis whose symptoms are restlessness, an unmotivated and undirected rage, sinking at times into vapid listlessness. This neurotic syndrome is intensified by the prevailing sense of insecurity. The threat of atomic war has corrupted our faith in life itself.

This universal neurosis has developed with the progress of technology. It is the neurosis of men whose chief expenditure of energy is to pull a lever or push a button, of men who have ceased to make things with their hands. Such inactivity applies not only to muscles and nerves but to the creative processes that once engaged the mind. If one could contrast visually, by time-and-motion studies, the daily actions of an eighteenth-century carpenter with a twentieth-century machinist, the latter would appear as a <u>confined, repetitive clot</u>, the former as a free and even fantastic pattern. But the most significant contrast could not be visualized—the contrast between a mind suspended aimlessly above an autonomous movement and a mind consciously bent on the shaping of a material substance according to the persistent evidence of the senses.

19. A suitable title for the above passage would be
    A. INCREASING PRODUCTION BY MEANS OF SYSTEMATIZATION
    B. LACK OF A SENSE OF CREATIVENESS AND ITS CONSEQUENCE
    C. TECHNOLOGICAL ACHIEVEMENT IN MODERN SOCIETY
    D. WHAT CAN BE DONE ABOUT SENSELESS VIOLENCE

19.____

20. According to the author, Shakespeare treated violence as a
    A. basically sinful act not in keeping with religious thinking
    B. just punishment of transgressors against moral law
    C. means of achieving dramatic excitement
    D. solution to a problem provided no other solution was available

20.____

21. According to the author, boredom may lead to
    A. a greater interest in leisure-time activities
    B. chronic fatigue
    C. senseless anger
    D. the acceptance of a job which does not provide a sense of creativity

21.____

22. The underlined phrase refers to the
    A. hand movements made by the carpenter
    B. hand movements made by the machinist
    C. relative ignorance of the carpenter
    D. relative ignorance of the machinist

22.____

23. The concentration of women and female-headed families in the city is both cause and consequence of the city's fiscal woes. Women live in cities because it is easier and cheaper for them to do so, but because fewer women are employed, and those that are receive lower pay than men, they do not make the same contribution to the tax base that an equivalent population of men would. Concomitantly, they are more dependent on public resources, such as transportation and housing. For these reasons alone, urban finances would be improved by increasing women's employment opportunities and pay. Yet nothing in our current urban policy is specifically geared to improving women's financial resources. There are some proposed incentives to create more jobs, but not necessarily ones that would utilize the skills women currently have. The most innovative proposal was a tax credit for new hires from certain groups with particularly high unemployment rates. None of the seven targeted groups were women.
    Which sentence is BEST supported by the above paragraph?
    A. Innovative programs are rapidly improving conditions for seven targeted groups with traditionally high unemployment rates.
    B. The contribution of women to a city's tax base reflects their superior economic position.
    C. Improving the economic position of women who live in cities would help the financial conditions of the cities themselves.
    D. Most women in this country live in large cities.

23.____

24. None of this would be worth saying if Descartes had been right in positing a one-to-one correspondence between stimuli and sensations. But we know that nothing of the sort exists. The perception of a given color can be evoked by an infinite number of differently combined wavelengths. Conversely, a given stimulus can evoke a variety of sensations, the image of a duck in one recipient, the image of a rabbit in another. Nor are responses like these entirely innate. One can learn to discriminate colors or patterns which were indistinguishable prior to training. To an extent still unknown, the production of data from stimuli is a learned procedure. After the learning process, the same stimulus evokes a different datum. I conclude that, though data are the minimal elements of our individual experience, they need be shared responses to a given stimulus only within the membership of a relatively homogeneous community: educational, scientific, or linguistic.
Which sentence is BEST supported by the above paragraph?
   A. One stimulus can give rise to a number of different sensations.
   B. There is a one-to-one correspondence between stimuli and sensations.
   C. It is not possible to produce data from stimuli by using a learned procedure.
   D. It is not necessary for a group to be relatively homogeneous in order to share responses to stimuli.

24.____

25. Workers who want to move in the direction of participative structures will need to confront the issues of power and control. The process of change needs to be mutually shared by all involved, or the outcome will not be a really participative model. The demand for a structural redistribution of power is not sufficient to address the problem of change toward a humanistic, as against a technological, workplace. If we are to change our institutional arrangements from hierarchy to participation, particularly in our workplaces, we will need to look to transformations in ourselves as well. As long as we are imbued with the legitimacy of hierarchical authority, with the sovereignty of the status quo, we will never be able to generate the new and original forms that we seek. This means if we are to be equal to the task of reorganizing our workplaces, we need to think about how we can reeducate ourselves and become aware of our assumptions about the nature of our social life together. Unless the issue is approached in terms of these complexities, I fear that all the worker participation and quality of work life efforts will fail.
According to the above paragraph, which of the following is NOT true?
   A. Self-education concerning social roles must go hand in hand with workplace reorganization.
   B. The structural changing of the workplace, alone, will not bring about the necessary changes in the quality of work life.
   C. Individuals can easily overcome their attitudes towards hierarchical authority.
   D. Changing the quality of work life will require the participation of all involved.

25.____

KEY (CORRECT ANSWERS)

1.	D	11.	A
2.	D	12.	D
3.	B	13.	C
4.	B	14.	A
5.	A	15.	C
6.	C	16.	D
7.	D	17.	C
8.	B	18.	D
9.	A	19.	B
10.	B	20.	B

21. C
22. B
23. C
24. A
25. C

READING COMPREHENSION
UNDERSTANDING AND INTERPRETING
WRITTEN MATERIAL

EXAMINATION SECTION

TEST 1

DIRECTIONS: Each question or incomplete statement is followed by several suggested answers or completions. Select the one that BEST answers the question or completes the statement. *PRINT THE LETTER OF THE CORRECT ANSWER IN THE SPACE AT THE RIGHT.*

In its current application to art, the term *"primitive"* is as vague and unspecific as the term "heathen" is in its application to religion. A heathen sect is simply one which is not affiliated with one or another of three or four organized systems of theology. Similarly, a primitive art is one which flourishes outside the small number of cultures which we have chosen to designate as civilizations. Such arts differ vastly and it is correspondingly difficult to generalize about them. Any statements which will hold true for such diverse aesthetic experiences as the pictographs of the Australians, the woven designs of the Peruvians, and the abstract sculptures of the African tribes must be of the broadest and simplest sort. Moreover, the problem is complicated by the meaning attached to the term "primitive" in its other uses. It stands for something simple, undeveloped, and, by implication, ancestral to more evolved forms. Its application to arts and cultures other than our own is an unfortunate heritage from the nineteenth-century scientists who laid the foundations of anthropology. Elated by the newly enunciated doctrines of evolution, these students saw all cultures as stages in a single line of development and assigned them to places in this series on the simple basis of the degree to which they differed from European culture, which was blandly assumed to be the final and perfect flower of the evolutionary process. This idea has long since been abandoned by anthropologists, but before its demise it diffused to other social sciences and became a part of the general body of popular misinformation. It still tinges a great deal of the thought and writing about the arts of non-European peoples and has been responsible for many misunderstandings.

1. The MAIN purpose of the passage is to   1._____
   A. explain the various definitions of the term "primitive"
   B. show that the term "primitive" can be applied validly to art
   C. compare the use of the term "primitive" to the use of the term "heathen"
   D. deprecate the use of the term "primitive" as applied to art
   E. show that "primitive" arts vary greatly among themselves

2. The nineteenth-century scientists believed that the theory of evolution   2._____
   A. could be applied to the development of culture
   B. was demonstrated in all social sciences
   C. was substantiated by the diversity of "primitive" art
   D. could be applied only to European culture
   E. disproved the idea that some arts are more "primitive" than others

3. With which of the following would the author agree?
   A. The term "primitive" is used only by the misinformed.
   B. "Primitive" arts may be as highly developed as "civilized" arts.
   C. The arts of a culture often indicated how advanced that culture was.
   D. Australian, Peruvian, and African tribal arts are much like the ancestral forms from which European art evolved.
   E. A simple culture is likely to have a simple art.

4. According to the author, many misunderstandings have been caused by the belief that
   A. most cultures are fundamentally different
   B. inferior works of art in any culture are "primitive" art
   C. "primitive" arts are diverse
   D. non-European arts are diverse
   E. European civilization is the final product of the evolutionary process

KEY (CORRECT ANSWERS)

1. D
2. A
3. B
4. E

TEST 2

DIRECTIONS: Each question or incomplete statement is followed by several suggested answers or completions. Select the one that BEST answers the question or completes the statement. *PRINT THE LETTER OF THE CORRECT ANSWER IN THE SPACE AT THE RIGHT.*

One of the ways the intellectual *avant-garde* affects the technical intelligentsia is through the medium of art, and art is, if only implicitly, a critique of experience. The turning upon itself of modern culture in the forms of the new visual art, the utilization of the detritus of daily experience to mock that experience, constitutes a mode of social criticism. Pop art, it is true, does not go beyond the surface of the visual and tactile experience of an industrial (and a commercialized) culture. Dwelling on the surface, it allows its consumers to mock the elements of their daily life, without abandoning it. Indeed, the consumption of art in the organized market for leisure serves at times to encapsulate the social criticism of the *avant-garde*. However, the recent engagement of writers, artists, and theater people in contemporary issues suggests that this sort of containment may have begun to reach its limits.

In an atmosphere in which the intellectually dominant group insists on the contradictions inherent in daily experience, the technical intelligentsia will find it difficult to remain unconscious of those contradictions. The technical intelligentsia have until now avoided contradictions by accepting large rewards for their expertise. As expertise becomes increasingly difficult to distinguish from ordinary service on the one hand, and merges on the other with the change of the social environment, the technical intelligentsia's psychic security may be jeopardized. Rendering of labor services casts it back into spiritual proletarianization; a challenge to the social control exercised by elites, who use the technical intelligentsia's labor power, pushes it forward to social criticism and revolutionary politics. That these are matters, for the moment, of primarily spiritual import does not diminish their ultimate political significance. A psychological precondition for radical action is usually far more important than an "objectively" revolutionary situation—whatever that may be.

The chances for a radicalization of the technical intelligentsia, thus extending the student revolt cannot be even approximated. I believe I have shown there is a chance.

1. It may be *inferred* that the technical intelligentsia are
   I. The executives and employers in society
   II. Critics of *avant-garde* art
   III. Highly skilled technical workers
   The CORRECT answer is:
   A. I only   B. I and III   C. I, II, and III
   D. III only   E. I and II

2. The engagement of the intellectual *avant-garde* in contemporary issues
   A. indicates that people tire of questioning the contradictions inherent in day-to-day living
   B. indicates that the technical intelligentsia are close to the point where they will rebel against the *avant-garde*
   C. could cause a challenge to the social control of the elites
   D. could cause the public to become more leisure-oriented
   E. could cause an increase in the consumption of art in the organized market for leisure services

3. The *possible* effect of the intellectual *avant-garde* on the technical intelligentsia is that
   A. the intellectual *avant-garde* makes the technical intelligentsia conscious of society's contradictions
   B. rapid curtailment of large rewards for expertise will result
   C. it may cause a strong likelihood of a radicalization of the technical intelligentsia
   D. the *avant-garde* will replace the employment of the technical intelligentsia in contemporary issues
   E. the rendering of labor services will be eliminated

4. If it is assumed that the technical intelligentsia becomes fully aware of the contradictions of modern life, it is the author's position that
   A. revolution will result
   B. the technical intelligentsia may refuse to perform manual labor
   C. the technical intelligentsia will be pushed forward to social criticism and revolutionary politics
   D. the technical intelligentsia will experience some psychic dislocation
   E. ordinary service will replace technical expertise

5. According to the author,
   A. the state of mind of a particular group may have more influence on its action than the effect of environmental factors
   B. the influence of art will often cause social upheaval
   C. matters of primarily spiritual import necessarily lack political significance
   D. the detritus of day-to-day living should be mocked by the intellectual *avant-garde*
   E. the technical intelligentsia can only protect their psychic security by self-expression through art

6. With which of the following would the author agree?
   I. As contradictions are less contained, the psychic security of all members of the working class would be jeopardized.
   II. The expertise of the technical intelligentsia evolved from the ownership and management of property.
   III. The technical intelligentsia is not accustomed to rendering labor services.
   The CORRECT answer is:
   A. I only   B. III only   C. I and III
   D. II only   E. None of the above

7. The MAIN purpose of the passage is to
   A. discuss the influence of the *avant-garde* art form on the expertise of the technical intelligentsia
   B. discuss the effect of the intellectual *avant-garde* on the working classes
   C. discuss the social significance of the technical intelligentsia
   D. discuss the possible effects of the de-encapsulation of *avant-garde* social criticism
   E. point out that before a change psychological preconditions are first established

KEY (CORRECT ANSWERS)

1. D   5. A
2. C   6. B
3. A   7. D
4. D

———

TEST 3

DIRECTIONS: Each question or incomplete statement is followed by several suggested answers or completions. Select the one that BEST answers the question or completes the statement. *PRINT THE LETTER OF THE CORRECT ANSWER IN THE SPACE AT THE RIGHT.*

Turbulent flow over a boundary is a complex phenomenon for which there is no really complete theory even in simple laboratory cases. Nevertheless, a great deal of experimental data has been collected on flows over solid surfaces, both in the laboratory and in nature, so that, from an engineering point of view at least, the situation is fairly well understood. The force exerted on a surface varies with the roughness of that surface and approximately with the square of the wind speed at some fixed height above it. A wind of 10 meters per second (about 20 knots, or 22 miles per hour) measured at a height of 10 meters will produce a force of some 30 tons per square kilometer on a field of mown grass or of about 70 tons per square kilometer on a ripe wheat field. On a really smooth surface, such as glass, the force is only about 10 tons per square kilometer.

When the wind blows over water, the whole thing is much more complicated. The roughness of the water is not a given characteristic of the surface but depends on the wind itself. Not only that, the elements that constitute the roughness—the waves—themselves move more or less in the direction of the wind. Recent evidence indicates that a large portion of the momentum transferred from the air into the water goes into waves rather than directly into making currents in the water; only as the waves break, or otherwise lose energy, does their momentum become available to generate currents, or produce Ekman layers. Waves carry a substantial amount of both energy and momentum (typically about as much as is carried by the wind in a layer about one wavelength thick), and so the wave-generation process is far from negligible. A violently wavy surface belies its appearance by acting, as far as the wind is concerned, as though it were very smooth. At 10 meters per second, recent measurements seem to agree, the force on the surface is quite a lot less than the force over mown grass and scarcely more than it is over glass; some observations in light winds of two or three meters per second indicate that the force on the wavy surface is less than it is on a surface as smooth as glass. In some way the motion of the waves seems to modify the airflow so that air slips over the surface even more freely than it would without the waves. This seems not to be the case at higher wind speeds, above about five meters per second, but the force remains strikingly low compared with that over other natural surfaces.

One serious deficiency is the fact that there are no direct observations at all in those important cases in which the wind speed is greater than about 12 meters per second and has had time and fetch (the distance over water) enough to raise substantial waves. The few indirect studies indicate that the apparent roughness of the surface increases somewhat under high-wind conditions, so that the force on the surface increases rather more rapidly than as the square of the wind speed.

Assuming that the force increases at least as the square of the wind speed, it is evident that high-wind conditions produce effects far more important than their frequency of occurrence would suggest. Five hours of 60-knot storm winds will put more momentum into the water than a week of 10-knot breezes. If it should be shown that, for high winds, the force on the surface increases appreciably more rapidly than as the square of the wind speed, then the transfer of momentum to the ocean will turn out to be dominated by what happens during the occasional storm rather than by the long-term average winds.

1. According to the passage, several hours of storm winds (60 miles per hour) over the ocean would
   A. be similar to the force exerted by light winds for several hours over glass
   B. create an ocean roughness which reduces the force exerted by the high winds
   C. have proved to be more significant in creating ocean momentum than light winds
   D. create a force not greater than 6 times the force of a 10-mile-per-hour wind
   E. eventually affect ocean current

2. According to the passage, a rough-like ocean surface
   A. is independent of the force of the wind
   B. has the same force exerted against it by high and light winds
   C. is more likely to have been caused by a storm than by continuous light winds
   D. nearly always allows airflow to be modified so as to cause the force of the wind to be less than on glass
   E. is a condition under which the approximate square of wind speed can never be an accurate figure in measuring the wind force

3. The author indicates that, where a hurricane is followed by light winds of 10 meters per second or less,
   I. ocean current will be unaffected by the light winds
   II. ocean current will be more affected by the hurricane winds than the following light winds
   III. the force of the light winds on the ocean would be less than that exerted on a wheat field.
   The CORRECT combination is:
   A. I only   B. III only   C. II and III   D. I and III   E. II only

4. The MAIN purpose of the passage is to discuss
   A. oceanic momentum and current
   B. turbulent flow of wind over water
   C. wind blowing over water as related to causing tidal flow
   D. the significance of high wind conditions on ocean momentum
   E. experiments in wind force

5. The author would be incorrect in concluding that the transfer of momentum to the ocean is dominated by the occasional storm if
   A. air momentum went directly into making ocean current
   B. high speed winds slipped over waves as easily as low speed winds
   C. waves did not move in the direction of wind
   D. the force exerted on a wheat field was the same as on mown grass
   E. the force of wind under normal conditions increased as the square of wind speed

6. A wind of 10 meters per second measured at a height of 10 meters will produce a force close to 30 tons per square mile on which of the following? 6.____
   A. Unmown grass
   B. Mown grass
   C. Glass
   D. Water
   E. A football field

KEY (CORRECT ANSWERS)

1. E
2. C
3. C
4. B
5. B
6. A

TEST 4

DIRECTIONS: Each question or incomplete statement is followed by several suggested answers or completions. Select the one that BEST answers the question or completes the statement. *PRINT THE LETTER OF THE CORRECT ANSWER IN THE SPACE AT THE RIGHT.*

Political scientists, as practitioners of a negligibly formalized discipline, tend to be accommodating to formulations and suggested techniques developed in related behavioral sciences. They even tend, on occasion, to speak of psychology, sociology, and anthropology as "hard core sciences." Such a characterization seems hardly justified. The disposition to uncritically adopt into political science non-indigenous sociological and general systems concepts tends, at times, to involve little more than the adoption of a specific, and sometimes barbarous, academic vocabulary which is used to redescribe reasonably well-confirmed or intuitively-grasped low-order empirical generalizations.

At its worst, what results in such instances is a runic explanation, a redescription in a singular language style, i.e., no explanation at all. At their best, functional accounts as they are found in the contemporary literature provide explanation sketches, the type of elliptical explanation characteristic of historical and psychoanalytic accounts. For each such account there is an indeterminate number of equally plausible ones, the consequence of either the complexity of the subject matter, differing perspectives, conceptual vagueness, the variety of sometimes mutually exclusive empirical or quasi-empirical generalizations employed, or syntactical obscurity, or all of them together.

Functional explanations have been most reliable in biology and physiology (where they originated) and in the analysis of servo mechanical and cybernetic systems (to which they have been effectively extended). In these areas we possess a well-standardized body of lawlike generalizations. Neither sociology nor political science has as yet the same resource of well-confirmed lawlike statements. Certainly sociology has few more than political science. What passes for functional explanation in sociology is all too frequently parasitic upon suggestive analogy and metaphor, trafficking on our familiarity with goal-directed systems.

What is advanced as "theory" in sociology is frequently a non-theoretic effort at classification or "codification," the search for an analytic conceptual schema which provides a typology or a classificatory system serviceable for convenient storage and ready retrieval of independently established empirical regularities. That such a schema takes on a hierarchic and deductive character, imparting to the collection of propositions a *prima facie* theoretical appearance, may mean no more than that the terms employed in the high-order propositions are so vague that they can accommodate almost any inference and consequently can be made to any conceivable state of affairs.

1. The author *implies* that, when the political scientist is at his best, his explanations   1.____
    A. are essentially a retelling of events
    B. only then form the basis of an organized discipline
    C. plausibly account for past occurrences
    D. are prophetic of future events
    E. are confirmed principles forming part of the political scientist's theory

2. With which of the following would the author probably agree?
   I. Because of an abundance of reasonable explanations for past conduct, there is the possibility of contending schools within the field of political science developing.
   II. Political science is largely devoid of predictive power.
   III. Political science has very few verified axioms.
   The CORRECT answer is:
   A. III only   B. I and III   C. I and II   D. I, II, III   E. I only

3. The passage *implies* that many sociological theories
   A. are capable of being widely applied to various situations
   B. do not even appear to be superficially theoretical in appearance
   C. contrast with those of political science in that there are many more confirmed lawlike statements
   D. are derived from deep analysis and exhaustive research
   E. appear theoretical but are really very well proved

4. The author's thesis would be UNSUPPORTABLE if
   A. the theories of the political scientist possessed predictive power
   B. political science did not consist of redescription
   C. political scientists were not restricted to "hard core sciences"
   D. political science consisted of a body of theories capable of application to any situation
   E. none of the above

5. The author believe that sociology as a "hard core science," contains reliable and functional explanations
   A. is never more than a compilation of conceptual schema
   B. is in nearly every respect unlike political science
   C. is a discipline which allows for varied inferences to be drawn from its general propositions
   D. is a science indigenous *prima facie* theoretical appearance containing very little codification posing as theory

KEY (CORRECT ANSWERS)

1. C
2. D
3. A
4. A
5. D

TEST 5

DIRECTIONS: Each question or incomplete statement is followed by several suggested answers or completions. Select the one that BEST answers the question or completes the statement. *PRINT THE LETTER OF THE CORRECT ANSWER IN THE SPACE AT THE RIGHT.*

    James' own prefaces to his works were devoted to structural composition and analytics and his approach in those prefaces has only recently begun to be understood. One of his contemporary critics, with the purest intention to blame, wrote what might be recognized today as sophisticated praise when he spoke of the later James as "an impassioned geometer" and remarked that "what interested him was not the figures but their relations, the relations which alone make pawns significant." James's explanations of his works often are so bereft of interpretation as to make some of our own austere defenses against interpretation seem almost embarrassingly rich with psychological meanings. They offer, with a kind of brazen unselfconsciousness, an astonishingly artificial, even mechanical view of novelistic invention. It's not merely that James asserts the importance of technique; more radically, he tends to discuss character and situation almost entirely as functions of technical ingenuities. The very elements in a Jamesian story which may strike us as requiring the most explanation are presented by James either as a *solution* to a problem of compositional harmony or else as the *donnee* about which it would be irrelevant to ask any questions at all.
    James should constantly be referred to as a model of structuralist criticism. He consistently redirects our attention from the referential aspect of a work of art (its extensions into "reality") to its own structural coherence as the principal source of inspiration.
    What is most interesting about James's structurally functional view of character is that a certain devaluation of what we ordinarily think of as psychological interest is perfectly consistent with an attempt to portray reality. It's as if he came to feel that a kind of autonomous geometric pattern, in which the parts appeal for their value to nothing but their contributive place in the essentially abstract pattern, is the artist's most successful representation of life. Thus, he could perhaps even think that verisimilitude—a word he liked—has less to do with the probability of the events the novelist describes than with those processes, deeply characteristic of life, by which he creates sense and coherence from any event. The only faithful picture of life in art is not in the choice of a significant subject (James always argues against the pseudo realistic prejudice), but rather in the illustration of sense- or design-making processes. James proves the novel's connection with life by deprecating its derivation from life; and it's when he is most abstractly articulating the growth of a structure that James is almost most successfully defending the mimetic function of art (and of criticism). His deceptively banal position that only execution matters means most profoundly that verisimilitude, properly considered, is the grace and the truth of a formal unity.

1. The author suggests that James, in explanations of his own art,   1.____
   A. was not bound by formalistic strictures but concentrated on verisimilitude
   B. was deeply psychological and concentrated on personal insight
   C. felt that his art had a one-to-one connection with reality
   D. was basically mechanical and concentrated on geometrical form
   E. was event-and-character-oriented rather than technique-oriented

2 (#5)

2. The passage indicates that James's method of approaching reality was
   A. that objective reality did not exist and was patterned only by the mind
   B. that formalism and pattern were excellent means of approaching reality
   C. not to concentrate on specific events but rather on character development
   D. that the only objective reality is the psychological processes of the mind
   E. that in reality events occur which are not structured but rather as random occurrences

2.____

3. The MAIN purpose of the paragraph is to
   A. indicate that James's own approach to his work is only now beginning to be understood
   B. deprecate the geometrical approach towards the novel
   C. question whether James's novels were related to reality
   D. indicate that James felt that society itself could be seen as a geometric structure
   E. discuss James's explanation of his works

3.____

4. In discussing his own works, James
   I. talks of people and events as a function of technique to the exclusion of all else
   II. is quick to emphasize the referential aspect of the work
   III. felt that verisimilitude could be derived not from character but rather from the ordering of event
   The CORRECT answer is:
   A. I only   B. II only   C. III only   D. I and III   E. I and II

4.____

5. The author
   A. *approves* of James's explanations of his work but *disapproves* his lack of discussion into the psychological makings of his characters
   B. *disapproves* of James's explanation of his own work and his lack of discussion into the psychological makings of his characters
   C. *approves* of James's explanations of his works in terms of structure as being well-rated to life
   D. *disapproves* of James's explanation of his works in terms of structure as lacking verisimilitude
   E. *approves* of James's explanation of his works because of the significance of the subjects chosen

5.____

6. The following is NOT true of James's explanation of his own works: He
   A. did not explain intriguing elements of a story except as part of a geometric whole
   B. felt the artist could represent life by its patterns rather than its events
   C. defended the imitative function of art by detailing the growth of a structure
   D. attempted to give the reader insight into the psychology of his characters by insuring that his explanation followed a strict geometrical pattern
   E. was able to devalue psychological interest and yet be consistent with an attempt to truly represent life

6.____

7. James believed it to be *essential* to 7.____
   A. carefully choose a subject which would lend itself to processes by which sense and cohesion is achieved
   B. defend the mimetic function of art by emphasizing verisimilitude
   C. emphasize the manner in which different facets of a story could fit together
   D. explain character in order to achieve literary harmony
   E. be artificial and unconcerned with representing life

KEY (CORRECT ANSWERS)

1.	D	5.	C
2.	B	6.	D
3.	E	7.	C
4.	C		

TEST 6

DIRECTIONS: Each question or incomplete statement is followed by several suggested answers or completions. Select the one that BEST answers the question or completes the statement. *PRINT THE LETTER OF THE CORRECT ANSWER IN THE SPACE AT THE RIGHT.*

The popular image of the city as it is now is a place of decay, crime, of fouled streets, and of people who are poor or foreign or odd. But what is the image of the city of the future? In the plans for the huge redevelopment projects to come, we are being shown a new image of the city. Gone are the dirt and the noise—and the variety and the excitement and the spirit. That it is an ideal makes it all the worse; these bleak new utopias are not bleak because they have to be; they are the concrete manifestation—and how literally—of a deep, and at times arrogant, misunderstanding of the function of the city.

Being made up of human beings, the city is, of course, a wonderfully resilient institution. Already it has reasserted itself as an industrial and business center. Not so many years ago, there was much talk of decentralizing to campus-like offices, and a wholesale exodus of business to the countryside seemed imminent. But a business pastoral is something of a contradiction in terms, and for the simple reason that the city is the center of things because it is a center, the suburban heresy never came off. Many industrial campuses have been built, but the overwhelming proportion of new office building has been taking place in the big cities. But the rebuilding of downtown is not enough; a city deserted at night by its leading citizens is only half a city. If it is to continue as the dominant cultural force in American life, the city must have a core of people to support its theatres and museums, its shops and its restaurants—even a Bohemia of sorts can be of help. For it is the people who like living in the city who make it an attraction to the visitors who don't. It is the city dwellers who support its style; without them there is nothing to come downtown to.

The cities have a magnificent opportunity. There are definite signs of a small but significant move back from suburbia. There is also evidence that many people who will be moving to suburbia would prefer to stay in the city—and it would not take too much more in amenities to make them stay. But the cities seem on the verge of muffing their opportunity and muffing it for generations to come. In a striking failure to apply marketing principles and an even more striking failure of aesthetics, the cities are freezing on a design for living ideally calculated to keep everybody in suburbia. These vast, barracks-like superblocks are not designed for people who like cities, but for people who have no other choice. A few imaginative architects and planners have shown that redeveloped blocks don't have to be repellent to make money, but so far their ideas have had little effect. The institutional approach is dominant, and, unless the assumptions embalmed in it are re-examined, the city is going to be turned into a gigantic bore.

1. The author would NOT be pleased with
    A. a crowded, varied, stimulating city
    B. the dedication of new funds to the reconstruction of the cities
    C. a more detailed understanding of the poor
    D. the elimination of assumptions which do not reflect the function of the city
    E. the adoption of a laissez-faire attitude by those in charge of redevelopment

1.____

2. "The rebuilding of downtown" (1st sentence, 3rd paragraph) refers to
   A. huge redevelopment projects to come
   B. the application of marketing and aesthetic principles to rejuvenating the city
   C. keeping the city as the center of business
   D. attracting a core of people to support the city's functions
   E. the doing away with barracks-like structures

3. According to the author the city, in order to better itself, *must*
   A. increase its downtown population
   B. attract an interested core of people to support its cultural institutions
   C. adhere to an institutional approach rather than be satisfied with the status quo
   D. erect campus-like business complexes
   E. establish an ideal for orderly future growth

4. The MAIN purpose of the passage is to
   A. show that the present people inhabiting the city do not make the city viable
   B. discuss the types of construction which should and should not take place in the city's future
   C. indicate that imaginative architects and planners have shown that redeveloped areas don't have to be ugly to make money
   D. discuss the human element in the city
   E. point out the lack of understanding by many city planners of the city's functions

5. The author's thesis would be LESS supportable if
   I. city planners presently understood that stereotyped reconstruction is doomed to ultimate failure
   II. the institutional approach referred to in the passage was based upon assumptions which took into account the function of the city
   III. there were signs that a shift back to the city from suburbia were occurring
   The CORRECT answer is:
   A. II only   B. II and III   C. I and II   D. I only   E. III only

KEY (CORRECT ANSWERS)

1. D
2. C
3. B
4. E
5. C

TEST 7

DIRECTIONS: Each question or incomplete statement is followed by several suggested answers or completions. Select the one that BEST answers the question or completes the statement. *PRINT THE LETTER OF THE CORRECT ANSWER IN THE SPACE AT THE RIGHT.*

In estimating the child's conceptions of the world, the first question is to decide whether external reality is as external and objective for the child as it is for adults. In other words, can the child distinguish the self from the external world? So long as the child supposes that everyone necessarily thinks like himself, he will not spontaneously seek to convince others, nor to accept common truths, nor, above all, to prove or test his opinions. If his logic lacks exactitude and objectivity, it is because the social impulses of mature years are counteracted by an innate egocentricity. In studying the child's thought, not in this case in relation to others but to things, one is faced at the outset with the analogous problem of the child's capacity to dissociate thought from self in order to form an objective conception of reality.

The child, like the uncultured adult, appears exclusively concerned with things. He is indifferent to the life of thought and the originality of individual points of view escape him. His earliest interests, his first games, his drawings are all concerned solely with the imitation of what is. In short, the child's thought has every appearance of being exclusively realistic.

But realism is of two types, or, rather, objectivity must be distinguished from realism. Objectivity consists in so fully realizing the countless intrusions of the self in everyday thought and the countless illusions which result—illusions of sense, language, point of view, value, etc.—that the preliminary step to every judgment is the effort to exclude the intrusive self. Realism, on the contrary, consists in ignoring the existence of self and thence regarding one's own perspective as immediately objective and absolute. Realism is thus anthropocentric illusion, finality—in short, all those illusions which teem in the history of science. So long as thought has not become conscious of self, it is a prey to perpetual confusions between objective and subjective, between the real and the ostensible; it values the entire content of consciousness on a single lane in which ostensible realities and the unconscious interventions of the self are inextricably mixed. It is thus not futile, but, on the contrary, indispensable to establish clearly and before all else the boundary the child draws between the self and the external world.

1. The result of a child's not learning that others think differently than he does is that   1.____
    A. the child will not be able to function as an adult
    B. when the child has matured, he will be innately egocentric
    C. when the child has matured, his reasoning will be poor
    D. upon maturity, the child will not be able to distinguish thought from objects
    E. upon maturity, the child will not be able to make non-ego-influenced value

2. Objectivity is the ability to   2.____
    A. distinguish ego from the external world
    B. dissociate oneself from others
    C. realize that others have a different point of view
    D. dissociate ego from thought

3. When thought is not conscious of self,
   A. one is able to draw the correct conclusions from his perceptions
   B. the apparent may not be distinguishable from the actual
   C. conscious thought may not be distinguishable from the unconscious
   D. the ego may influence the actual
   E. ontogeny recapitulates phylogony

4. The MAIN purpose of the passage is to
   A. argue that the child should be made to realize that others may not think like he does
   B. estimate the child's conception of the world
   C. explain the importance of distinguishing the mind from external objects
   D. emphasize the importance of non-ego-influenced perspective
   E. show how the child establishes the boundary between himself and the external world

5. The author *implies* that, if an adult is to think logically,
   A. his reasoning, as he matures, must be tempered by other viewpoints
   B. he must be able to distinguish one physical object from another
   C. he must be exclusively concerned with thought instead of things
   D. he must be able to perceive reality without the intrusions of the self
   E. he must not value the content of consciousness on a single plain

6. Realism, according to the passage, is
   A. the realization of the countless intrusions of the self
   B. final and complete objectivity
   C. a desire to be truly objective and absolute
   D. the ability to be perceptive and discerning
   E. none of the above

7. The child who is exclusively concerned with things
   A. thinks only objectivity
   B. is concerned with imitating the things he sees
   C. must learn to distinguish between realism and anthropomorphism
   D. has no innate ability
   E. will, through interaction with others, often prove his opinions

KEY (CORRECT ANSWERS)

1. C   5. A
2. E   6. E
3. B   7. B
4. D

TEST 8

DIRECTIONS: Each question or incomplete statement is followed by several suggested answers or completions. Select the one that BEST answers the question or completes the statement. *PRINT THE LETTER OF THE CORRECT ANSWER IN THE SPACE AT THE RIGHT.*

Democracy is not logically antipathetic to most doctrines of natural rights, fundamental or higher law, individual rights, or any similar ideals—but merely asks citizens to take note of the fact that the preservation of these rights rests with the majority, in political processes, and does not depend upon a legal or constitutional Maginot line. Democracy may, then, be supported by believers in individual rights providing they believe that rights—or any transcendental ends—are likely to be better safeguarded under such a system. Support for democracy on such instrumental ground may, of course, lead to the dilemma of loyalty to the system vs. loyalty to a natural right—but the same kind of dilemma may arise for anyone, over any prized value, and in any political system, and is insoluble in advance.

There is unanimous agreement that—as a matter of fact and law, not of conjecture—no single right can be realized, except at the expense of other rights and claims. For that reason their absolute status, in some philosophic sense, is of little political relevance. Political policies involve much more than very generable principles or rights. The main error of the older natural rights school was not that it had an absolute right, but that it had too many absolute rights. There must be compromise, and, as any compromise destroys the claim to absoluteness, the natural outcome of experience was the repudiation of all of them. And now the name of "natural right" can only creep into sight with the reassuring placard, "changing content guaranteed." Nor is it at all easy to see how many doctrine of inalienable, natural, individual rights can be reconciled with a political doctrine of common consent—except in an anarchist society, or one of saints. Every natural right ever put forward, and the lists are elusive and capricious, is every day invaded by governments, in the public interest and with widespread public approval.

To talk of relatively attainable justice or rights in politics is not to plump for a moral relativism—in the sense that all values are equally good. But while values may be objective, the specific value judgments and policies are inevitably relative to a context, and is only when a judgment divorces context from general principle that it looks like moral relativism. Neither, of course, does the fact of moral diversity invalidate all moral rules.

Any political system, then, deals only with relatively attainable rights, as with relative justice and freedoms. Hence, we may differ in given instances on specific policies, despite agreement on broad basic principles such as a right or a moral "ought"; and, per contra, we may agree on specific policies while differing on fundamental principles or long-range objectives or natural rights. Politics and through politics, law and policies, give these rights—and moral principles—their substance and limits. There is no getting away from the political nature of this or any other prescriptive ideal in a free society.

1. With which of the following would the author *agree*?   1._____
    A. Natural and individual rights can exist at all only under a democracy.
    B. While natural rights may exist, they are only relatively attainable.
    C. Civil disobedience has no place in a democracy where natural rights have no philosophic relevance.
    D. Utilitarianism, which draws its criteria from the happiness and welfare of individuals, cannot logically be a goal of a democratic state.
    E. Some natural rights should never be compromised for the sake of political policy.

2. It can be *inferred* that a democratic form of government
   A. can be supported by natural rightists as the best pragmatic method of achieving their aims
   B. is a form of government wherein fundamental or higher law is irrelevant
   C. will inn time repudiate all inalienable rights
   D. forces a rejection of moral absolutism
   E. will soon exist in undeveloped areas of the world

3. The MAIN purpose of the passage is to
   A. discuss natural rights doctrine
   B. compare and contrast democracy to individual rights
   C. discuss the reconciliation of a doctrine of inalienable natural rights with a political system
   D. discuss the safeguarding of natural rights in a democratic society
   E. indicate that moral relativism is antipathetic to democracy

4. The author indicates that natural rights
   I. are sometimes difficult to define
   II. are easily definable but at times unreconcilable with a system of government predicated upon majority rule
   III. form a basis for moral relativism
   The CORRECT answer is:
   A. I only   B. II only   C. I and II   D. III only   E. II and III

5. The fact that any political system deals with relatively attainable rights
   A. shows that all values are equally good or bad
   B. is cause for divorcing political reality from moral rules
   C. shows that the list of natural rights is elusive and capricious
   D. is inconsistent with the author's thesis
   E. does not necessarily mean that natural rights do not exist

6. The passage indicates that an important conflict which can exist in a democracy is the rights of competing groups, i.e., labor versus management
   A. adherence to the democratic process versus non-democratic actions by government
   B. difficulty in choosing between two effective compromises
   C. adherence to the democratic process versus the desire to support a specific right
   D. difficulty in reconciling conflict by natural rights

KEY (CORRECT ANSWERS)

1. B   4. A
2. A   5. E
3. C   6. D

PREPARING WRITTEN MATERIAL
EXAMINATION SECTION
TEST 1

DIRECTIONS: Each short paragraph below is followed by four restatements or summaries of the information contained within it. Select the one that most completely and accurately restates the information given in the paragraph. *PRINT THE LETTER OF THE CORRECT ANSWER IN THE SPACE AT THE RIGHT.*

1. India's night jasmine, or hurshinghar, is different from most flowering plants, in that its flowers are closed during the day, and open after dark. The scientific reason for this is probably that the plant has avoided competing with other flowers for pollinating insects and birds, and relies instead on the service of nocturnal bats that are drawn to the flower's nectar. According to an old Indian legend, however, the flowers sprouted from the funeral ashes of a beautiful young girl who had fallen hopelessly in love with the sun.
    A. Despite the Indian legend that explains why the hurshinghar's flowers open at dusk, scientists believe it has to do with competition for available pollinators.
    B. The Indian hurshinghar's closure of its flowers during the day is due to a lack of available pollinators.
    C. The hurshinghar of India has evolved an unhealthy dependency on nocturnal bats.
    D. Like most myths, the Indian legend of the hurshinghar's night-flowering has been disproved by science.

1._____

2. Charles Lindbergh's trans-Atlantic flight from New York to Paris made him an international hero in 1927, but he lived nearly another fifty years, and by most accounts they weren't terribly happy ones. The two greatest tragedies of his life—the 1932 kidnapping and murder of his oldest son, and an unshakeable reputation as a Nazi sympathizer during World War II—he blamed squarely on the rabid media hounds who stalked his every move.
    A. Despite the fact that Charles Lindbergh had a hand in the two greatest tragedies of his life, he insisted on blaming the media for his problems.
    B. Charles Lindbergh lived a largely unhappy life after the glory of his 1927 trans-Atlantic flight, and he blamed his unhappiness on media attention
    C. Charles Lindbergh's later life was marked by despair and disillusionment.
    D. Because of the rabid media attention sparked by Charles Lindbergh's 1927 trans-Atlantic flight, he would later consider it the last happy event of his life

2._____

3. The United States, one of the world's youngest nations in the early twentieth century, had yet to spread its wings in terms of foreign affairs, preferring to remain isolated and opposed to meddling in the affairs of others. But the fact remained that as a young nation situated on the opposite side of the globe from Europe, Africa, and Asia, the United States had much work to do in

3._____

establishing relations with the rest of the world. So, too, as the European colonial powers continued to battle for influence in North and South America, did the United States come to believe that it was proper for them to keep these nations from encroaching into their sphere of influence.
- A. The roots of the Monroe Doctrine can be traced to the foreign policy shift of the United States during the early nineteenth century.
- B. In the early nineteenth century, the United States shifted its foreign policy to reflect a growing desire to actively protect its interests in the Western Hemisphere.
- C. In the early nineteenth century, the United States was too young and undeveloped to have devised much in the way of foreign policy.
- D. The United States adopted a more aggressive foreign policy in the early nineteenth century in order to become a diplomatic player on the world stage.

4. Hertha Ayrton, a nineteenth-century Englishwoman, pursued a career in science during a time when most women were not given the opportunity to go to college. Her series of successes led to her induction into the Institution of Electrical Engineers in 1899, when she was the first woman to receive this professional honor. Her most noted accomplishment was the research and invention of an anti-gas fan that the British War Office used in the trench warfare of World War I. 4._____
- A. The British Army's success in World War I can be partly attributed to Hertha Ayrton, a groundbreaking British scientist.
- B. Hertha Ayrton was the first woman to be inducted into the Institution of Electrical Engineers.
- C. The injustices of nineteenth-century England were no match for the brilliant mind of Hertha Ayrton.
- D. Hertha Ayrton defied the restrictions of her society by building a successful scientific career.

5. Scientists studying hyenas in Tanzania's Ngorongoro Crater have observed that hyena clans have evolved a system of territoriality that allows each clan a certain space to hunt within the 100-square-mile area. These territories are not marked by natural boundaries, but by droppings and excretions from the hyenas' scent glands. Usually, the hyenas take these boundary lines very seriously; some hyena clans have been observed abandoning their pursuit of certain prey after the prey has crossed into another territory, even though no members of the neighboring clan are anywhere in sight. 5._____
- A. The hyenas of Ngorongoro Crater illustrate that the best way to peacefully co-exist within a limited territory is to strictly delineate and defend territorial borders.
- B. While most territorial boundaries are marked using geographical features, the hyenas of Ngorongoro Crater have devised another method.
- C. The hyena clans of Ngorongoro Crater, in order to co-exist within a limited hunting territory, have developed a method of marking strict territorial boundaries.
- D. As with most species, the hyenas of Ngorongoro Crater have proven the age-old motto: "To the victor go the spoils."

3 (#1)

6. The flood control policy of the U.S. Army Corps of Engineers has long been an obvious feature of the American landscape—the Corps seeks to contain the nation's rivers with an enormous network of dams and levees, "channelizing" rivers into small, confined routes that will stay clear of settled flood—plains when rivers rise. As a command of the U.S. Army, the Corps seems to have long seen the nation's rivers as an enemy to be fought; one of the agency's early training films speaks of the Corps' "battle" with its adversary, Mother Nature.

   A. The dams and levees built by the U.S. Army Corps of Engineers have at least defeated their adversary, Mother Nature.
   B. The flood control policy of the U.S. Army Corps of Engineers has often reflected a military point of view, making the nation's rivers into enemies that must be defeated.
   C. When one realizes that the flood policy of the U.S. Army Corps of Engineers has always relied on a kind of military strategy, it is only possible to view the Corps' efforts as a failure.
   D. By damming and channelizing the nation's rivers, the U.S. Army Corps of Engineers have made America's flood plains safe for farming and development.

6.____

7. Frogs with extra legs or missing legs have been showing up with greater frequency over the past decade, and scientists have been baffled by the cause. Some researchers have concluded that pesticide runoff from farms is to blame; others say a common parasite, the trematode, is the culprit. Now, a new study suggests that both these factors in combination have disturbed normal development in many frogs, leading to the abnormalities.

   A. Despite several studies, scientists still have no idea what is causing the widespread incidence of deformities among aquatic frogs.
   B. In the debate over what is causing the increase in frog deformities, environmentalists tend to blame pesticide runoff, while others blame a common parasite, the trematode.
   C. A recent study suggests that both pesticide runoff and natural parasites have contributed to the increasing rate of deformities in frogs.
   D. Because of their aquatic habitat, frogs are among the most susceptible organisms to chemical ad environmental change, and this is illustrated by the increasing rate of physical deformities among frog populations.

7.____

8. The builders of the Egyptian pyramids, to insure that each massive structure was built on a completely flat surface, began by cutting a network of criss-crossing channels into the pyramid's mapped-out ground space and partly filling the channels with water. Because the channels were all interconnected, the water was distributed evenly throughout the channel system, and all the workers had to do to level their building surface was cut away any rock above the waterline.

   A. The modern carpenter's level uses a principle that was actually invented several centuries ago by the builders of the Egyptian pyramids.
   B. The discovery of the ancient Egyptians' sophisticated construction techniques is a quiet argument against the idea that they were built by slaves.

8.____

C. The use of water to insure that the pyramids were level mark the Egyptians as one of the most scientifically advanced of the ancient civilizations.
D. The builders of the Egyptian pyramids used a simple but ingenious method for ensuring a level building surface with interconnected channels of water

9. Thunderhead Mountain, a six-hundred-foot-high formation of granite in the Black Hills of South Dakota, is slowly undergoing a transformation that will not be finished for more than a century, when what remains of the mountain will have become the largest sculpture in the world. The statue, begun in 1947 by a Boston Sculptor named Henry Ziolkowski, is still being carved and blasted by his wife and children into the likeness of Crazy Horse, the legendary chief of the Sioux tribe of American natives. The enormity of the sculpture—the planned length of one of the figure's arms is 263 feet—is understandable, given the historical greatness of Crazy Horse.   9.____
    A. Only a hero as great as Crazy Horse could warrant a sculpture so large that it will take morae than a century to complete.
    B. In 1947, sculptor Henry Ziolkowski began work on what he imagined would be the largest sculpture in the world—even though he knew he would not live to see it completed.
    C. The huge Black Hills sculpture of the great Sioux chief Crazy Horse, still being carried out by the family of Henry Ziolkowski, will some day be the largest sculpture in the world.
    D. South Dakota's Thunderhead Mountain will soon be the site of the world's largest sculpture, a statue of the Sioux chief Crazy Horse.

10. Because they were some of the first explorers to venture into the western frontier of North America, the French were responsible for the naming of several native tribes. Some of these names were poorly conceived—the worst of which was perhaps Eskimo, the name for the natives of the far North, which translates roughly as "eaters of raw flesh." The name is incorrect; these people have always cooked their fish and game, and they now call themselves the Inuit, a native term that means "the people."   10.____
    A. The first to explore much of North America's western frontier were the French, and they usually gave improper or poorly-informed names to the native tribes.
    B. The Eskimos of North America have never eaten raw flesh, so it is curious that the French would give them a name that means "eaters of raw flesh."
    C. The Inuit have fought for many years to overcome the impression that they eat raw flesh.
    D. Like many native tribes, the Inuit were once incorrectly named by French explorers, but they have since corrected the mistake themselves.

11. Of the 30,000 species of spiders worldwide, only a handful are dangerous to human beings, but this doesn't prevent many people from having a powerful fear of all spiders, whether they are venomous or not. The leading scientific theory about arachnophobia, as this fear is known, is that far in our evolutionary past, some species of spider must have presented a serious enough threat to people that the sight of a star-shaped body or an eight-legged walk was coded into our genes as a danger signal.

11.____

    A. Scientists theorize that peoples' widespread fear of spiders can be traced to an ancient spider species that was dangerous enough to trigger this fearful reaction.
    B. The fear known as arachnophobia is triggered by the sight of a star-shaped body or an eight-legged walk.
    C. Because most spiders have a uniquely shaped body that triggers a human fear response, many humans are afflicted with the fear of spiders known as arachnophobia.
    D. Though only a few of the planet's 30,000 spider species are dangerous to people, many people have an unreasonable fear of them.

12. From the 1970s to the 1990s, the percentage of Americans living in the suburbs climbed from 37% to 47%. In the latter part of the 1990s, a movement emerged that questioned the good of such a population shift—or at least, the good of the speed and manner in which this suburban land was being developed. Often, people began to argue, the planning of such growth was flawed, resulting in a phenomenon that has become known as suburban "sprawl," or the growth of suburban orbits around cities at rates faster than infrastructures could support, and in ways that are damaging to the environment

12.____

    A. The term "urban sprawl" was coined in the 1990s, when the movement against unchecked suburban development began to gather momentum.
    B. In the 1980s and 1990s, home builders benefited from a boom in their most favored demographic segment, suburban new home buyers.
    C. Suburban development tends to suffer from poor planning, which can lead to a lower quality of life for residents
    D. The surge in suburban residences in the late twentieth century was criticized by many as "sprawl" that could not be supported by existing resources

13. Medicare, a $200 billion-a-year program, processes 1 billion claims annually, and in the year 2000, the computer system that handles these claims came under criticism. The General Accounting Office branded Medicare's financial management system as outdated and inadequate—one in a series of studies and reports warning that the program is plagued with duplication, overcharges, double billings, and confusion among users.

13.____

    A. The General Accounting Office's 2000 report proves that Medicare is bloated bureaucracy in need of substantial reform.
    B. Medicare's confusing computer network is an example of how the federal government often neglects the programs that mean the most to average American citizens.

C. In the year 2000, the General Accounting Office criticized Medicare's financial accounting network as inefficient and outdated.
D. Because it has to handle so many claims each year, Medicare's financial accounting system often produces redundancies and errors.

14. The earliest known writing materials were thin clay tablets, used in Mesopotamia more than 5,000 years ago. Although the tablets were cheap and easy to produce, they had two major disadvantages: they were difficult to store, and once the clay had dried and hardened, a person could not write on them. The ancient Egyptians later discovered a better writing material—the thin bark of the papyrus reed, a plant that grew near the mouth of the Nile River, which could be peeled into long strips, woven into a mat-like layer, pounded flat with heavy mallets, and then dried in the sun. 14.____
    A. The Egyptians, after centuries of frustration with clay writing tablets, were finally forced to invent a better writing surface.
    B. With the bark of the papyrus reed, ancient Egyptians made a writing material that overcame the disadvantages of clay tablets.
    C. The Egyptian invention of the papyrus scroll was necessitated in part by a relative lack of available clay.
    D. The word "paper" can be traced to the innovations of the Egyptians, who made the first paper-like writing material from the bark of papyrus plant.

15. In 1850, the German pianomaker Heinrich Steinweg and his family stepped off an immigrant ship in New York City, threw themselves into competition with dozens of other established craftsmen, and defeated them all by reinventing the instrument. The company they created commanded the market for nearly the next century and a half, while their competitors—some of the most acclaimed pianomakers in the business—faded into obscurity. And all the while, Steinway & Sons, through their sponsorship and encouragement of the world's most distinguished pianists, helped define the cultural life of the young United States. 15.____
    A. The Steinways capitalized on weak competition during the mid-nineteenth century to capture the American piano market.
    B. Because of their technical and cultural innovations, the Steinways had an advantage over other American pianomakers.
    C. Heinrich Steinweg founded the Steinway piano empire in 1850.
    D. From humble immigrant origins, the Steinway family rose to dominate both the pianomaking industry and American musical culture.

16. Feng Shui, the ancient Chinese science of studying the natural environment's effect on a person's well-being, has gained new popularity in the design and decoration of buildings. Although a complex area of study, a basic premise of Feng Shui is that each building creates a unique field of energy which affects the inhabitants of that building or home. In recent years, decorators and realtors have begun to offer services which include a diagnosis of a building's Feng Shui, or energy. 16.____
    A. Feng Shui, the Chinese science of balancing environmental energies, has been given more aesthetic quality by recent practitioners.

B. Generally, practitioners of Feng Shui work to create balance within a room, carefully arranging sharp and soft surfaces to create a positive environment that suits the room's primary purpose.
C. The idea behind the Chinese "science" of Feng Sui objects give off certain energies that affect a building's inhabitants has been a difficult one for most Westerners to accept, but it is gaining in popularity.
D. The ancient Chinese science of Feng Shui, which studies the balance of energies in a person's environment, has become popular among those who design and decorate buildings.

17. Because the harsh seasonal variations of the Kansas plains make survival difficult for most plant life, the area is dominated by tall, sturdy grasses. The only tree that has been able to survive and prosper throughout the wide expanse of prairie is the cottonwood, which can take root and grow in the most extreme climatic conditions. Sometimes a storm will shear off a living branch and carry it downstream, where it may snag along a sandbar and take root.   17.____
    A. Among the plant life of the Kansas plains, the only tree is the cottonwood.
    B. The only prosperous tree on the Kansas plains is the cottonwood, which can take root and grow in a wide range of conditions.
    C. Only the cottonwood, whose branches can grow after being broken off and washed down a river, is capable of surviving the climatic extremes of the Kansas plains.
    D. Because it is the most widespread and hardiest tree on the Kansas plains, the cottonwood had become a symbol of pioneer grit and fortitude.

18. In the twenty-first century, it's easy to see the automobile as the keystone of American popular culture. Subtract linen dusters, driving goggles, and women's *crepe de chine* veils from our history, and you've taken the Roaring out of the Twenties. Take away the ducktail haircuts, pegged pants, and upturned collars from the teen Car Cult of the Fifties, and the decade isn't nearly as Fabulous. Were the chromed and tailfinned muscle cars of the automobile' Golden Age modeled after us, or were we mimicking them?   18.____
    A. Ever since its invention, the automobile has shaped American culture.
    B. Many of the familiar names we give historical era, such as "Roaring Twenties" and "Fabulous Fifties," were given because of the predominance of the automobile.
    C. Americans' tastes in clothing have been determined primarily by the cars they drive.
    D. Teenagers have had a fascination for automobiles ever since the motorcar was first invented.

19. Since the 1960s, an important issue for Canada has been the status of minority French-speaking Canadians, especially in the province of Quebec, whose inhabitants make up 30% of the Canadian population and trace their ancestry back to a Canada that preceded British influence. In response to pressure from Quebec nationalists, the government in 1982 added a Charter of Rights to the constitution, restoring important rights that dated back to the time of aboriginal treaties. Separatism is still a prominent issue, though successive   19.____

referendums and constitutional inquiries have not resulted in any realistic progress toward Quebec's independence.
   A. Despite the fact that Quebec's inhabitants have their roots in Canada's original settlers, they have been constantly oppressed by the descendants of those who came later, the British.
   B. It seems unavoidable that Quebec's linguistic and cultural differences with the rest of Canada will some day lead to its secession.
   C. French-speaking Quebec's activism over the last several decades has led to concessions by the Canadian government, but it seems that Quebec will remain a part of the country for some time.
   D. The inhabitants of Quebec are an aboriginal culture that has been exploited by the Canadian government for years, but they are gradually winning back their rights.

20. For years, musicians and scientists have tried to discover what it is about an eighteenth-century Stradivarius violin—which may sell for more than $1 million on today's market—that gives it its unique sound. In 1977, American scientist Joseph Nagyvary discovered that the Stradivarius is made of a spruce wood that came from Venice, where timber was stored beneath the sea, and unlike the dry-seasoned wood from which other violins were made, this spruce contains microscopic holes which add resonance to the violin's sound. Nagyvary also found the varnish used on the Stradivarius to be equally unique, containing tiny mineral crystals that appear to have come from ground-up gemstones, which would filter out high-pitched tones and give the violin a smoother sound.   20.____
   A. After carefully studying Stradivarius violins to discover the source of their unique sound, an American scientist discovered two qualities in the construction of them that set them apart from other instruments: the wood from which they were made, and the varnish used to coat the wood.
   B. The two qualities that give the Stradivarius violin such a unique sound are the wood, which adds resonance, and the finish, which filters out high-pitched tones.
   C. The Stradivarius violin, because of the unique wood and finish used in its construction, is widely regarded as the finest string instrument ever manufactured in the world.
   D. A close study of the Stradivarius violin has revealed that the best wood for making violins is Venetian spruce, stored underwater.

21. People who watch the display of fireflies on a clear summer evening are actually witnessing a complex chemical reaction called "bioluminescence," which turns certain organisms into living light bulbs. Organisms that produce this light undergo a reaction in which oxygen combines with a chemical called lucerfin and an enzyme called luciferase. Depending on the organism, the light produced from this reaction can range from the light green of the firefly to the bright red spots of a railroad worm.   21.____
   A. Although the function of most displays of bioluminescence is to attract mates, as is the case with fireflies, other species rely on bioluminescence for different purposes.

B. Bioluminescence, a phenomenon produced by several organisms, is the result of a chemical reaction that takes place within the body of the organism.
C. Of all the organisms in the world, only insects are capable of displaying bioluminescence.
D. Despite the fact that some organisms display bioluminescence, these reactions produce almost no heat, which is why the light they create is sometimes referred to as cold light.

22. The first of America's "log cabin" presidents, Andrew Jackson rose from humble backcountry origins to become a U.S. congressman and senator, a renowned military hero, and the seventh president of the United States. Among many Americans, especially those of the western frontier, he was acclaimed as a symbol of the "new" American: self-made, strong through closeness to nature, and endowed with a powerful moral courage.   22.____
    A. Andrew Jackson was the first American president to rise from modest origins.
    B. Because he was born poor, President Andrew Jackson was more popular among Americans of the western frontier.
    C. Andrew Jackson's humble background, along with his outstanding achievements, made him into a symbol of American strength and self-sufficiency.
    D. Andrew Jackson achieved success as a legislator, soldier, and president because he was born humbly and had to work for every honor he ever received.

23. In the past few decades, while much of the world's imagination has focused on the possibilities of outer space, some scientists have been exploring a different frontier—the ocean floor. Although ships have been sailing the oceans for centuries, only recently have scientists developed vehicles strong enough to sustain the pressure of deep-sea exploration and observation. These fiberglass vehicles, called submersibles, are usually just big enough to take two or three people to the deepest parts of the oceans' floors.   23.____
    A. Modern submersible vehicles, thanks to recent technological innovations, are now exploring underwater cliffs, crevices, and mountain ranges that were once unreachable.
    B. While most people tend to fantasize about exploring outer space, they should be turning toward a more accessible realm—the depths of the earth's oceans.
    C. Because of the necessarily small size of submersible vehicles, exploration of the deep ocean is not a widespread activity.
    D. Recent technological developments have helped scientists to turn their attention from deep space to the deep ocean.

24. The panda—a native of the remote mountainous regions of China—subsists almost entirely on the tender shoots of the bamboo plant. This restrictive diet has allowed the panda to evolve an anatomical structure that is completely different from that of other bears, whose paws are aligned for running, stabbing, and scratching. The panda's paw has an over-developed wrist bone that juts out below the other claws like a thumb, and the panda uses this "thumb" to grip bamboo shoots while it strips them of their leaves.
    A. The panda is the only bear-like animal that feeds on vegetation, and it has a kind of thumb to help it grip bamboo shoots.
    B. The panda's limited diet of bamboo has led it to evolve a thumb-like appendage for grasping bamboo shoots.
    C. The panda's thumb-like appendage is a factor that limits its diet to the shoots of the bamboo plant.
    D. Because bamboo shoots must be held tightly while eaten, the panda's thumb-like appendage ensure that it is the only bear-like animal that eats bamboo.

25. The stability and security of the Balkan region remains a primary concern for Greece in post-Cold War Europe, and Greece's active participation in peacekeeping and humanitarian operations in Georgia, Albania, and Bosnia are substantial examples of this commitment. Due to its geopolitical position, Greece believes it necessary to maintain, at least for now, a more nationalized defense force than other European nations. It is Greece's hope that the new spirit of integration and cooperation will help establish a common European foreign affairs and defense policy that might ease some of these regional tensions, and allow a greater level of Greek participation in NATO's integrated military structure.
    A. Greece's proximity to the unstable Balkan region has led it to keep a more nationalized military, though it hopes to become more involved in a common European defense force.
    B. The Balkan states present a greater threat to Greece than any other European nation, and Greece has adopted a highly nationalist military force as a result.
    C. Greece, the only Balkan state to belong to NATO, has an isolationist approach to defense, but hopes to achieve greater integration in the organization's combined forces.
    D. Greece's failure to become more militarily integrated with the rest of Europe can be attributed to the failure to establish a common European defense policy.

KEY (CORRECT ANSWERS)

1.	A	11.	A
2.	B	12.	D
3.	B	13.	C
4.	D	14.	B
5.	C	15.	D
6.	B	16.	D
7.	C	17.	B
8.	D	18.	A
9.	C	19.	C
10.	D	20.	A

21. B
22. C
23. D
24. B
25. A

PREPARING WRITTEN MATERIAL

PARAGRAPH REARRANGEMENT
COMMENTARY

The sentences that follow are in scrambled order. You are to rearrange them in proper order and indicate the letter choice containing the correct answer at the space at the right.

Each group of sentences in this section is actually a paragraph presented in scrambled order. Each sentence in the group has a place in that paragraph; no sentence is to be left out. You are to read each group of sentences and decide upon the best order in which to put the sentences so as to form a well-organized paragraph.

The questions in this section measure the ability to solve a problem when all the facts relevant to its solution are not given.

More specifically, certain positions of responsibility and authority require the employee to discover connection between events sometimes, apparently, unrelated. In order to do this, the employee will find it necessary to correctly infer that unspecified events have probably occurred or are likely to occur. This ability becomes especially important when action must be taken on incomplete information.

Accordingly, these questions require competitors to choose among several suggested alternatives, each of which presents a different sequential arrangement of the events. Competitors must choose the MOST logical of the suggested sequences.

In order to do so, they may be required to draw on general knowledge to infer missing concepts or events that are essential to sequencing the given events. Competitors should be careful to infer only what is essential to the sequence. The plausibility of the wrong alternatives will always require the inclusion of unlikely events or of additional chains of events which are NOT essential to sequencing the given events.

It's very important to remember that you are looking for the best of the four possible choices, and that the best choice of all may not even be one of the answers you're given to choose from.

There is no one right way to solve these problems. Many people have found it helpful to first write out the order of the sentences, as they would have arranged them, on their scrap paper before looking at the possible answers. If their optimum answer is there, this can save them some time. If it isn't, this method can still give insight into solving the problem. Others find it most helpful to just go through each of the possible choices, contrasting each as they go along. You should use whatever method feels comfortable and works for you.

While most of these types of questions are not that difficult, we've added a higher percentage of the difficult type, just to give you more practice. Usually there are only one or two questions on this section that contain such subtle distinctions that you're unable to answer confidently. And you then may find yourself stuck deciding between two possible choices, neither of which you're sure about.

EXAMINATION SECTION
TEST 1

DIRECTIONS: Each group of sentences in this section is actually a paragraph presented in scrambled order. Each sentence in the group has a place in that paragraph; no sentence is to be left out. You are to read each group of sentences so as to form a well-organized paragraph. Before trying to answer the questions which follow each group of sentences, jot down the correct order of the sentences. Then answer each of the questions by printing the letter of the correct answer in the space at the right. Remember that you will receive credit only for answers marked.

P. The awards to Eugene O'Neill, William Faulkner, and Ernest Hemingway were welcomed by all.
Q. Thereafter, in 1938 Pearl Buck won the prize.
R. Three of the six times that the Nobel Prize for Literature has been given to Americans, the choice has been universally approved.
S. Now, the award has gone to John Steinbeck.
T. But, in 1930, the prize went to Sinclair Lewis.

1. Which sentence did you put second
   A. P   B. Q   C. R   D. S   E. T

2. Which sentence did you put after Sentence S?
   A. P
   B. Q
   C. R
   D. T
   E. None of the above. Sentence S is last.

3. Which sentence did you put before Sentence Q?
   A. P
   B. R
   C. S
   D. T
   E. None of the above. Sentence Q is first.

4. Which sentence did you put first?
   A. P   B. Q   C. R   D. S   E. T

5. Which sentence did you put last?
   A. P   B. Q   C. R   D. S   E. T

KEY (CORRECT ANSWERS)

1. A
2. E
3. D
4. C
5. D

TEST 2

DIRECTIONS: Each group of sentences in this section is actually a paragraph presented in scrambled order. Each sentence in the group has a place in that paragraph; no sentence is to be left out. You are to read each group of sentences so as to form a well-organized paragraph. Before trying to answer the questions which follow each group of sentences, jot down the correct order of the sentences. Then answer each of the questions by printing the letter of the correct answer in the space at the right. Remember that you will receive credit only for answers marked.

P. Five months before he died, Herman Melville finished BILLY BUDD.
Q. Had he survived, Melville could have made BILLY BUDD as memorable and lucid awork as MOBY DICK.
R. Now, Peter Jones has written and directed a motion picture based on BILLY BUDD.
S. Unhappily, the film is a failure.
T. Several years ago, Robert Smith and Thomas Johnson
U. dramatized the book and brought it to the stage.

1. Which sentence did you put before Sentence Q?

   A. P
   B. R
   C. S
   D. T
   E. None of the above. Sentence Q is first.

2. Which sentence did you put after Sentence T?

   A. P
   B. Q
   C. R
   D. S
   E. None of the above. Sentence T is last.

3. Which sentence did you put after Sentence R?

   A. P
   B. Q
   C. S
   D. T
   E. None of the above. Sentence R is last.

4. Which sentence did you put before Sentence P?

   A. Q
   B. R
   C. S
   D. T
   E. None of the above. Sentence P is first.

5. Which sentence did you put first? 5._____
   A. P B. Q C. R D. S E. T

KEY (CORRECT ANSWERS)

1. A
2. C
3. C
4. E
5. A

TEST 3

DIRECTIONS: Each group of sentences in this section is actually a paragraph presented in scrambled order. Each sentence in the group has a place in that paragraph; no sentence is to be left out. You are to read each group of sentences so as to form a well-organized paragraph. Before trying to answer the questions which follow each group of sentences, jot down the correct order of the sentences. Then answer each of the questions by printing the letter of the correct answer in the space at the right. Remember that you will receive credit only for answers marked.

P. This spirit must occasionally find a direct outlet.
Q. The spirit of our culture is latent violence.
R. Hob violence will do perfectly as an outlet, however, since one cannot lose therespect of one's neighbors while they, too, are burning automobiles.
S. One must work within the spirit of his culture.
T. Murder will not do as a direct outlet, since it loses the respect of one's neighbors.

1. Which sentence did you put after Sentence R?

   A. P
   B. Q
   C. S
   D. T
   E. None of the above. Sentence R is last.

2. Which sentence did you put first?

   A. P   B. Q   C. R   D. S   E. T

3. Which sentence did you put after Sentence P?

   A. Q
   B. R
   C. S
   D. T
   E. None of the above. Sentence P is last.

4. Which sentence did you put after Sentence Q?

   A. P
   B. R
   C. S
   D. T
   E. None of the above. Sentence Q is last.

5. Which sentence did you put after Sentence S?

   A. P
   B. Q
   C. R
   D. T
   E. None of the above. Sentence S is last.

KEY (CORRECT ANSWERS)

1. E
2. D
3. D
4. A
5. B

TEST 4

DIRECTIONS: Each group of sentences in this section is actually a paragraph presented in scrambled order. Each sentence in the group has a place in that paragraph; no sentence is to be left out. You are to read each group of sentences so as to form a well-organized paragraph. Before trying to answer the questions which follow each group of sentences, jot down the correct order of the sentences. Then answer each of the questions by printing the letter of the correct answer in the space at the right. Remember that you will receive credit only for answers marked.

- P. A few years ago, Franz Schmidt was appointed Germany's Foreign Minister.
- Q. He had a Nazi background and was disliked intensely by the opposition.
- R. During these past years, however, Schmidt has silenced his critics and confounded the political prophets.
- S. He had also not been successful as Minister of the Interior.
- T. Schmidt had no particular qualifications for the position and several disadvantages.

1. Which sentence did you put first?
   A. P B. Q C. R D. S E. T

2. Which sentence did you put after Sentence S?
   A. P
   B. Q
   C. R
   D. T
   E. None of the above. Sentence S is last.

3. Which sentence did you put before Sentence Q?
   A. P
   B. R
   C. S
   D. T
   E. None of the above. Sentence Q is first.

4. Which sentence did you put after Sentence R?
   A. P
   B. Q
   C. S
   D. T
   E. None of the above. Sentence R is last.

5. Which sentence did you put before Sentence S?
   A. P
   B. Q
   C. R
   D. T
   E. None of the above. Sentence S is first.

TEST 4

KEY (CORRECT ANSWERS)

1. A
2. C
3. D
4. E
5. B

TEST 5

1. A
2. E
3. D
4. E
5. B

KEY (CORRECT ANSWERS)

1. A
2. E
3. D
4. E
5. B

---

www.ingramcontent.com/pod-product-compliance
Lightning Source LLC
Chambersburg PA
CBHW082211300426
44117CB00016B/2757